W9-BMF-571

PRAISE FOR GRIEF IS LOVE

"*Grief Is Love* is a remarkable homage about what it's like to love through loss. This gem of a book is like taking an exhale or being hugged or being told that everything is going to be all right and actually believing it. As I continue to navigate the loss of my father, which happened when I was a small child, I am reminded, with the help of this book, that grief doesn't have an expiration date. Every human should own this marvel of a book. I treasured every page, and I am indebted to it."

—Jennifer Pastiloff, national bestselling author of *On Being Human*

"This book, like its author, radiates empathy, rejects platitudes, and uplifts even while interrogating life's darkest crevices. In examining her own experiences with life-changing loss, Marisa helps us recognize the gift of love in grief and offers a guide for how to show up for those we love in the moments that matter most. Marisa knows grief, but she also knows deep joy, and she has laced both into every page of this exquisite book." —Alicia Menendez, MSNBC anchor and author of *The Likeability Trap*

"*Grief Is Love* is the rare project that reshapes all of our sensory expectations of catastrophe. In this particular season, I'm not sure I could have chosen a more useful and dynamic literary companion. This book will bolster faith in our community of grievers and help us accept communal care and love."

—Kiese Laymon, author of *Heavy* and winner of the Andrew Carnegie Medal

"This is a beautiful [book] about the love that lasts after loss. With powerful prose and refreshing candor, Marisa Renee Lee challenges the cultural stigma around grief and highlights a healthier way to cope. If you're struggling with loss, reading this book might just be a jolt of hope."

—Adam Grant, #1 *New York Times* bestselling author of *Think Again* and *Option B*

"Absolutely amazing. Marisa has transformed her own profound losses into a beautiful proclamation of the power of love. If you struggle with grief of any kind, this book will help you navigate it."

—Reshma Saujani, CEO of the Marshall Plan for Moms, founder of Girls Who Code, and *New York Times* bestselling author *Brave, Not Perfect*

GRIEF IS LOVE

GRIEF IS LOVE

Living with Loss

MARISA RENEE LEE

New York Boston

Legacy Lit, an imprint of Hachette Books
Hachette Book Group
1290 Avenue of the Americas, New York, NY 10104
LegacyLitBooks.com
twitter.com/LegacyLitBooks
instagram.com/LegacyLitBooks

First edition: April 2022

Published by Hachette Books, an imprint of Perseus Books, LLC, a subsidiary of Hachette Book Group, Inc. The Hachette Books and Legacy Lit name and logo is a trademark of the Hachette Book Group.

Print book interior design by Marie Mundaca

Library of Congress Cataloging-in-Publication Data

Names: Lee, Marisa Renee, author.
Title: Grief is love : living with loss / Marisa Renee Lee.
Description: New York : Legacy Lit, [2022] | Includes bibliographical references.
Identifiers: LCCN 2021053698 | ISBN 9780306926020 (hardcover) | ISBN 9780306926013 (ebook)
Subjects: LCSH: Grief. | Loss (Psychology) | Love.
Classification: LCC BF575.G7 L439 2022 | DDC 155.9/37—dc23/eng/20211229
LC record available at https://lccn.loc.gov/2021053698

ISBNs: 9780306926020 (hardcover), 9780306926013 (ebook)

Printed in the United States of America

LSC-C

Printing 1, 2022

For my mother, Lisa, who taught me everything I need to know about love.

The heart of the wise is in the house of mourning.

—Ecclesiastes 7:4

Contents

GRIEF IS LOVE

Grief Is Love

My mother lives in the water.

In the fluidity, the comfort, and the power of water is where I find her. I run to the water when things get hard. I can find her in a warm bath, in the fresh scent that emerges after a light spring rain, in the vastness and overwhelming power of the ocean. And just as I need water to live, I stubbornly refuse to live without the love of my mother. And you don't need to live without the love of your person either.

We are taught that grief is something that arrives in the immediate aftermath of death, and while that's certainly true, it's not the whole story. Grief is the experience of navigating your loss, figuring out how to deal with the absence of your loved one forever. It's understanding that the pain you feel because of their absence is because you've experienced a great love. That love doesn't end when they die, and you don't have to get over it. My hope in writing this book is to give those of us who know loss, and those who care to understand our experiences, a bit of guidance for living a full life after losing someone we love—a life where we can continue to love them, grieve them, and honor them on our terms. I've written what I wish I knew when I lost my mother fourteen years ago, and the many lessons I've learned since. As I sit writing this on October 18, 2021, the United States has lost more than 720,000 lives to COVID-19; globally, we've lost 4.5 million people to this pandemic. Like you and me, each of these people has left behind loved ones who are, for the first time, trying to figure out life after death. We can no longer afford to ignore grief, to relegate it to whispered conversations, to expect folks to navigate their brokenheartedness on their own. It is neither practical, nor possible, nor humane.

My mother, Lisa, took her last breath on February 28, 2008, ten days after turning forty-nine. I was with her when life left her body. I did the thing I had prepared for as her daughter and one of her caretakers, the thing I promised her: I ensured she died on her own terms, the way she wanted to, in our home. I was twenty-five, and it felt like the epitome of adulting, but what I didn't know, what no one told me, was that her death was also a beginning. Her death sparked a new life for me. At 5:37 p.m. that day in February, I was forced to start learning how to live without her, how to somehow live a full and joyful life, with a permanent hole in my heart.

When she died, I was unmoored. I was an adult in name only, and just as I was trying to sort through who I was and how I wanted to show up in the world, my sense of self was destroyed. Losing my mother meant losing myself too. Who would I be without my mother? We are irrevocably changed when we lose someone we love because so much of who we are is a reflection of the people who love us, and now one of those people is gone. In the beginning, the mere act of sustaining your own life feels impossible.

But I promised my mother I would be fine, so I "returned" to my life. The act of returning is often the hardest part. What does life look like without her, without my person? We don't know. But we push ourselves to do it anyway, sometimes by force.

And I am nothing if not the epitome of a strong Black woman, a type-A striver. I may as well have "I've got this" tattooed on my back. I returned to my job on Wall Street and my wannabe *Sex and the City* existence two weeks after my mom's death, and I did the thing Black women have been doing for centuries: I kept my mouth shut about the extent of my pain. As I attempted to cobble together the former pieces of myself with what was left, I thought it was normal to feel sad for perhaps the first few weeks. I didn't know it was normal to feel sad on and off for years, for what feels like it will be for the rest of my life. I didn't know anger, envy, frustration, depression, anxiety, and shame were common elements of grief. I did not understand the importance of grace and the need to extend it to myself and others. I had no idea that grief was actively impacting my body and my brain in ways that made maintaining my health, my career, and my relationships challenging.

I didn't know all these things were grief, and perhaps more importantly, I didn't know all of these things were normal, so I fought them, and I hid them, and I lied about them to myself and others. I assumed there was something wrong with me for having so many feelings about a dead mother. I was embarrassed and ashamed. So I did my best to keep my feelings to myself, if I even acknowledged them at all.

As I continued to move further and further away from that fateful day in February, I found myself mourning her death over and over again. Her absence and my loss seem to know no limits. I grieve for the relationship we could have had as adults, the relationship she would have had with my husband. The delicious new recipes we might have exchanged or an eye roll we might have shared at something ridiculous my dad just said. Her absence is particularly acute when shitty things happen in my life: an infertility diagnosis and loss of a much-wanted pregnancy, supporting my sister through her mental illness, fear in the midst of a global pandemic, the battles and anxieties that spark at the turn of a key daily in life. At one time I would have been able to call my mother, to ask for her advice, to hear the warmth of her voice. It's in these big and tiny corners of my life that I miss her every day.

When I lost my pregnancy, I was once again forced to confront the overwhelming pain and disorientation that arrive immediately following a loss. I learned that *grief is love.* I felt foolish for being upset over a bundle of cells, but then I realized I felt sorrow, not for these cells, but because of all the love and hope I held for this future child and my role as her mother. It wasn't about how far along the pregnancy was; it was about an imagined future that would never come to pass. And I yearned for my mother during those weeks and months because of the unconditional love, support, and comfort she provided to me throughout her life. Love serves as the foundation for our most intimate relationships, so of course we grieve when those we love are no longer here to love us in the ways we've come to expect. My desire to become a mother is inextricably connected to the love I have for my mother and the love she has for me. That love is a present-tense kind of love, not something that is stuck in the past. Even in death, she is mine.

Grief, like love, is also limitless, which means we have to find a way to live with it. To understand that it is your deep love for the person. Your loss is yours alone; no matter who you lost or when you lost them, you deserve to honor that love, you deserve to live a full life after death while still loving them. No one can tell you how to handle your resulting grief, but my goal in sharing my stories and missteps is to provide you with a sense of comfort and community, and maybe even an occasional smile. In addition to my many foibles and occasional lessons, I wanted to ensure this book was not just about me and my story, so it is also grounded in the leading research on grief and loss. Because everyone's experience with grief is different, do not use this book as a road map, or set of specific instructions. Instead, I hope it might serve as a compass to help you navigate your unique journey.

Marisa

1

. . . Permission

PERMISSION ISN'T A common word in discussions about grief, but it's what's been missing. Giving yourself permission to grieve is the beginning of the journey: permission to know that you have loved and cherished someone's life deeply and will continue to.

There comes a time when you have no choice. Permission to grieve becomes required.

You never understand just how useless you are as an individual, how mortal, how humane and powerless you are until you know that someone you love is dying, and there is absolutely nothing you can do to stop it from happening. The anticipation of a day you would do anything to prevent, but can't; it isn't just an emotional pain, it is all encompassing. This feeling is felt in your headaches, insomnia, body pains, stomachaches, loss of appetite, or an appetite for everything. I lost over twenty-five pounds the year before my mom died, and I didn't notice it, I just started wearing more belts. You are forced to exist in this tenuous space between life and death, and there is often an ominous undertone to everything. I remember what I call "the beginning" of my mom's death well, the moment when I knew that her life would one day end, that it was more than possible, it was a guarantee. It was an idea that I could never have mentally or emotionally fathomed, molded into a real thought before this time, though I had cared for her many years through her illness—but now it was happening.

"Can you feel that?" the doctor asked.

"Yes," she admitted. And just like that, my grief journey began.

It was a muggy afternoon in June, and I was supposed to be at college enjoying Senior Week festivities in advance of my graduation. Instead, I found myself standing in a corner furiously taking notes in a doctor's office in Fishkill, New York, with my mother, father, and godmother. Examination rooms are not made for that many additional guests, but I was determined at twenty-two to be the fourth adult in the room because I needed to know with certainty what exactly was wrong with my mother. She was lying faceup on the examination table wearing one of those ridiculous paper shirts. An orthopedic doctor, a family friend, had recently discovered cancer in her bones, but now this oncologist was touching her breasts. I knew just enough about cancer to know this was not good. My palms started to sweat. He gently lifted my mother's hand and placed it on her left breast and asked, "Can you feel that?", and she replied, "Yes." The floor opened up beneath my feet. The stability I had previously taken for granted was replaced by the pain that arrives when you learn that someone you love is going to die. It was a deep sense of foreboding, a bodily knowledge of things to come that you would do just about anything to avoid. I didn't have an understanding of what grief was or how it felt. After he removed her hand from her breast, my deepest fears were confirmed. He patiently explained that my mother had breast cancer that had already migrated to her bones. A death sentence. At the time, it felt foolish and, frankly, immature of me to be so upset about her future death while she was still with us, so I didn't give myself permission to grieve. I gave myself permission to step up and soldier on.

My mother had been sick with multiple sclerosis since I was thirteen. My sister has bipolar disorder. I had no idea what it might look like to give myself permission to be the needy one, permission to make a scene, permission to acknowledge just how quickly those four words, "Can you feel that?" broke my heart. I knew if cancer was in her bones that started in her breast, her diagnosis was stage 4: treatable but not curable. She was going to die soon. Instead of giving myself permission to feel anything, I shut my feelings off, and I stepped up to help my mom and dad like everyone expected me to.

After death isn't the only time to grieve. The period before death can be filled with anguish and all sorts of complicated feelings, and the only thing that makes grief—whether before or after death—even a tiny bit easier is giving yourself permission to grieve on *your terms.* Whether it arrives before death or a decade later, when you hold your newborn son in your arms and all you can see is your dead father's face, give yourself permission to feel grief, to experience the fullness of it, to let it break your heart or to let it make you smile. Grief is not solely limited to wailing, devastation, and pain. Grief can also be a laugh, a memory you share with a loved one recalling something your person said, or a joke about the time that your mom saved one friend's hair after another friend accidentally dyed it orange (true story, my mom did things like that even for my friends). Living with loss requires you to give yourself permission to grieve however you want to for the rest of your life...because grief is love, and both love and grief live on.

Permission to know it is okay to grieve is the freedom that we all need. Permission to remove, or at least reduce, any sense that "you've been too sad for too long," that you might not be "grieving right," or that you "aren't grieving often enough." Grief is deeply personal; you are the sole authority on how it should be done, and only you can grant yourself permission to experience grief. And you must make a decision to walk this path that your soul hungers to express. On your grief journey, begin by granting yourself consent to do it however you need to, to be whoever you need to be, to feel whatever you might feel. It will make living with loss easier, more bearable, and less burdensome.

The earlier that you start to give yourself permission to grieve, the better. Grief is never easy, but you can make it a little bit lighter.

If you are helping to care for your loved one or if you serve as a primary caretaker, there is a load of grief you must confront every day. There's not a place you can hide from it; it's in front of you. There's a constant reminder of their death sitting right in the task at hand that you must do for them. Often with this role come guilt and resentment. Guilt anytime you might complain about how challenging life is as a caretaker, because at least they are still here. Resentment toward anyone who doesn't have to balance the challenges that come with caretaking, with preparing for their death, all while managing the expectations of your "normal life." There is no bereavement policy that accounts for the time before death. As you mourn the inevitable, life goes on. Whether you are sitting with them in hospice care or at home, you're holding their hand in support; but there's also the burden of a broken heart that you're forced to carry quietly and the unending anxiety about a future without them. When is this thing going to actually happen? What is it going to be like to watch my person die? How do I ensure that when she does die, I have no regrets? What do I want to make sure I ask her or try to learn from her before it happens? What is going to happen to me when she's gone? How do I ensure that I don't lose my mind in the midst of all of this? So many questions without perfect answers, and generally very little time or support to tend to them. And in the absence of giving yourself permission to feel this burden that grief causes, you suffer silently.

It was often that my heart felt like it might explode out of my chest. It was not just a one-time occurrence. I was in a state of continuous free fall. My mind raced incessantly with questions after my mom's cancer diagnosis, and I just wanted it to stop, to be able to turn off what was happening to her and to me. What I truly wanted to do was stop time. I knew with each passing day, I was one day closer to losing my mother. I was trying to hold on to her like a child attempting to hold on to sand with fists clenched, grasping tight. What I would have loved to do was hold her with a cupped, nearly open palm, the way you might hold water, in recognition of the softness, the fluidity that love and death require. I didn't feel stable enough, secure enough, safe enough to let her go. I couldn't see a life lived without her. I couldn't envision a world in which she ceased to exist, but unfortunately, I was in a position where I'd have to anticipate it.

As her caretaker, I would have been described as high functioning. It's a strength of many caretakers, but oftentimes we're the folks who need to be most conscious about care. While my mom was dying, as I mentioned, I was working at a fancy job on Wall Street, managing a breast cancer charity in her honor, and frequenting all the cool bars in the West Village. Generally, I looked and behaved like a flippant twenty-something New Yorker. But I was a fucking mess. My anxiety was out of control. I started requiring medication to get through the day. I quickly outgrew the standard sleeping pills—Ambien and Lunesta—and graduated to a more complex, and unbeknownst to me, addictive, regimen of temazepam and Xanax to attempt to get some sleep. Even medicated, most nights I was lucky to get three or four hours of sleep. I was a wreck. I knew my mother was dying, and there was nothing I could do about it. The closer we got to her death, the greater my anxiety.

There was this heaviness that I simply couldn't shake. I would be fine for one portion of the day and then find myself wandering the streets of Soho weeping silently behind giant sunglasses so no one could tell. I cried often in the back of empty churches. I had a job that I loved and, minus my dying mother, a life that many would envy. Yet I could barely get out of bed some days.

One winter morning, I wrote in my journal, "I am in serious pain, emotional pain that is turning into physical pain, but not enough physical pain." I wanted to claw at my face. I wanted to jump in the near-frozen Hudson River. I wanted my body to feel pain, as that seemed to be the only thing that could even momentarily pause the mental anguish that I refused to fully reckon with.

I didn't know it was grief. I hadn't yet given myself permission to even acknowledge the feelings. I feared that if I gave myself permission to press pause and grieve, everything would fall apart, when in reality it was probably the one thing that would have made things a little easier.

No one told me this at the time, but pressing pause and giving yourself permission to experience the fullness of grief is what helps you move through the worst parts of it and learn to live with it.

Whether you're a witness to slow death or the death of your person was sudden, few people are going to actively encourage your grief, at least not after the funeral. Not because they don't love you, but because, as human beings, we have a natural inclination to do whatever we can to help people "shake off" negative emotions and move on to a more "positive" place. When people see you sad or brokenhearted or angry when grieving, they will be inclined to want to help fix it, to take it away. But sometimes that isn't possible. You should not feel guilty for your grieving. You love the person you lost or are losing, and grief will likely be with you in some form for the rest of your life.

We often feel guilt about grief because there is always this sense that we're not supposed to do it, we're not doing it enough or right, or we're doing it too much; but when you're grieving, nothing feels quite right. Give yourself permission to approach grief however it feels right to you, however it shows up. And because you are giving yourself the green light, or a free pass, to move through this pain however you want, you don't have to feel guilty if you don't cry at the funeral. Or if you fall apart in public weeks, months, or years later. You don't have to feel bad if you're angry at your person for leaving you.

You don't have to worry about whether or not it is okay to feel too many different feelings, because *it is all okay*. I think of permission as one of those physical hall passes you got as a kid in elementary school. If you had a hall pass, you knew you were covered if you were caught in the halls during class time by a teacher or, heaven forbid, the principal. A hall pass came with feelings of protection and even a little bit of entitlement. You almost wanted an adult to stop and ask you where you were going so you could show them that you were doing what you were supposed to be doing. You knew you were all good. There was this feeling of confidence connected to that little hall pass. That is how permission works in grief.

Before my mother's death and before cancer, I was only thirteen when my mother first got sick, and she never got better. It would take doctors years to reach a definitive diagnosis of multiple sclerosis. By the time she was diagnosed there were lesions on her brain. The disease had done permanent, irreversible damage to her body and mind. As a teenage caretaker, I was forced to grow up fast and to reckon with all of the aforementioned uncomfortable feelings. On top of all of that, I didn't have anyone to talk to about it. How could I complain about my mom whom I loved so deeply? I admitted only to myself that I hated the inconvenience of a sick parent, of a mother who could not always care for herself fully. It was also deeply painful watching her suffer. Instead of taking time to acknowledge how hard it was on me to have a sick parent, I tried to ignore it by becoming a mini-adult. It's not common thinking in our society yet to acknowledge our grief and give it attention. We keep quiet as we work through the shame of parking in that handicapped spot or doing our Sunday visit to the ICU. I'd unload a wheelchair and attempt to push my mother over the brick and cobblestone streets of Harvard Square when my parents came to visit me at college, knowing I was causing her discomfort. With every push, every stone, I experienced the sharpness of grief anew. This is the quiet part of grief that is often overlooked. The part that we don't allow ourselves space to process—we just push on through.

If I'd been honest about my grief as a teenager, I would have also admitted that I hated that everything could no longer just be about me. Self-centeredness is a fundamental part of a parent–child relationship, but as her caretaker I quickly learned to subjugate my needs to hers, and that's what we all do. That's what we feel is our greatest obligation and honor to them. I thought that I was selfish to have those thoughts. Once I wrote in my journal, "Selfishness is anything I do for myself that I could be doing for someone else." But I was wrong. I needed to give myself permission to understand that I was in pain too. Most of us are hardwired to take away the care for ourselves to give it to others—our loved one who is sick or disabled and suffering, or our family members who are also struggling because of it. It becomes our innate response to give and give and give. Permission to acknowledge what hurts feels selfish. I didn't feel worthy of prioritizing my feelings. My mother was dying, and any time not spent focused on her was selfish. As you know, this was not true; my mother would not have thought that, and neither would your person. Until the day she died, my mother experienced joy whenever she knew I was experiencing joy. We may think that our sacrifices make everything better or help our loved one get some sort of relief—as if there is some sort of tally, where if you suffer more, they will suffer less. I am here to tell you that is not how it works. Treating yourself like shit is not going to save your person, and it won't aid your grief.

Yet years later, as a young adult, when I stood in an oncologist's office in my hometown anxiously taking notes on my mother's cancer diagnosis, with my mom on that examination table, my needs and wants started to, often subconsciously, take a backseat even more so. The moment I learned what we thought was bone cancer was actually stage 4 breast cancer that had migrated throughout her skeletal system, something inside of me shifted. I started to really hear the doctor's words, like "treatable not curable." When he said "months to years," I understood the weight of his words, and that could mean any day now. Nothing was solid after that; everything was written in pencil. I was waiting for the worst to happen, and closer than ever to it. It's the thing that no one wants to speak about. The pending death hasn't happened yet, and you are expected to live like everything is normal, and it hurts.

I see you and I'm sorry. Many of us know what you could be experiencing at this very moment, either living or reliving it.

Everyone talks about Elisabeth Kübler-Ross's five stages of grief, but there is no stage for the lead-up. That expectant time period when you try to figure out how to do this impossible thing. How to say goodbye to someone you love—your spouse, your parent, heaven-forbid your child, your dear friend or relative. There is no meaningful societal support for any of it.

Our society struggles to deal with death, pain, suffering, illness, and loss. Given our inability to deal with death, we definitely do not have a culture for supporting someone going through it. In any given ICU, it's silent and sterile. That's why it's important to make the space for yourself. No one else can do it but you. It may make some people uncomfortable, but you deserve to take up space. Do whatever you need to do to get through it.

In my case, in an effort to channel my debilitating anxiety, I started "preparing" to lose my mother. I believed I could make it all easier by being organized and strategic. I created a three-pronged plan focused on making my mother's last days, however many she might have, as fun and germ-free as possible. I acted as though I were the CEO of my mother's death. In hindsight, my heart breaks for my twenty-four-year-old self. I believed I was capable of preparing myself to live without the woman who had raised me, but what I was really doing was coping the only way I knew how.

I built meticulous spreadsheets and to-do lists. I made friends with the local undertaker and told my father to increase my mother's life insurance policy. I ensured we always had copies of my mom's do-not-resuscitate orders and health care proxy forms on hand. I knew what she would wear when we buried her, down to the brand and color of her nail polish. When she suggested donating her organs and I reminded her they were riddled with cancer, she offered up her body for science instead. I knew everything, from what she wanted to happen to her body to the few things she owned. Every piece of jewelry, whether purchased by my father or by her on the Home Shopping Network, was accounted for.

I had even preemptively built a notification email list for my friends to inform my broader social group when she died. I was as prepared as they come, and completely delusional. I built a plan (with a lot of help) that ensured that my mother died on her terms and had a badass funeral. I was ready.

But I wasn't.

In those years right before I lost my mom, the closest I came to giving myself permission to grieve her illness was hiding in the stairwell at Vassar Brothers Medical Center. Only hospital staff use the stairs, and they are used to death and dying and grief, so generally they will leave you alone, which is exactly what I wanted. I'd sit there sobbing silently into my cheap black pashmina without anyone bothering me. I needed space to quietly mourn without feeling ashamed for having all of these damn feelings. This was my attempt to create space for my grief. I had no idea how good I was at hiding in public until I knew my mother was dying.

I had no other place to turn to release all of the hurt that was sitting on my chest, that had settled into my bones while watching her make jokes from her hospital bed and knowing that she might never come out of it. Grief consumed my mind, yet I couldn't give myself permission to release it without feeling ashamed. I didn't even understand that it was grief. I understood that I'd miss her, but I could not begin to understand what sat on the other side of her death. I only knew it would be devastating. It already was.

Then the day came.

I've told you about how that day, February 28, 2008, affected me, but it will forever be a day that I replay over and over again, as I'm sure you do with your day, the day you had to reckon with the loss of your person. It's a day that created a new existence and undid another, a death and unwanted rebirth.

My mom was having a bad day. At the time, she was at home using oxygen and receiving high doses of methadone, which is typically reserved for people who are coming off opioids, for pain. She was vomiting, and her breathing seemed labored, but given how long she had been sick and the things I'd seen over the years, none of this seemed all that out of the ordinary. She was still laughing with my grandparents and holding court in our living room as she always had. That Thursday simply felt like a typical bad day in the series of bad days we had experienced over the years.

That afternoon I got off the phone with one of her doctors, who suggested we try to get our hands on some marijuana. I shared this with my mom, and we both started cracking up at the idea of me, my parents, and my aunt, who was living with us at the time, all sitting around and smoking weed together. It just seemed so absurd to the two of us, especially since my Goody Two-shoes of a mother had never even smoked weed before. She laughed, and then she collapsed. I tried to catch her body, a body that had been bloated by chemotherapy drugs and steroids, while my own body had shrunken thanks to my grief and anxiety. As my dad called 911, I was left to support my mother's body. Because of my size, I had to use my entire body to hold her up. My arms wrapped around her, and in the shock of that moment, I still didn't think that was *the moment.* Then she started to seize. I felt her body shake so violently in my arms that I could no longer hold her. I laid her body on the floor.

My life changed in that moment; something inside of me broke. It's a piece of me that I no longer expect to get back.

When I looked down at her, I knew it was over. Her lifeless body in pale pink pajamas, lying on the floor, in the narrow space between my parents' bed and the wall. Life as I knew it ended. I screamed a scream that I didn't know I had in me. It was animalistic. It was a wail. I screamed with my entire body. I've never been that out of control before or since. When the moment of death arrives, it can feel like something has broken you wide open—because it has. There are no rules. There's no other way to describe it. It's a moment that shatters you. A moment that brings with it emotions and feelings—

physical, mental, and psychological—all in one suffocating wave. You have been destroyed. Give yourself permission to sit with this or any other feeling you have. There's no need to push back. There are no words that are strong enough to convey all that you have lost. And give yourself permission to have the greatest compassion for yourself.

Accept what comes in that moment and after—whether it's days, weeks, or years, give yourself permission to hold the depths of what you've experienced. Some people have to scream, others throw up, stand in silence, and it's all okay because the most unimaginable thing has happened to you. And the more you have loved, the greater the loss you will feel. You deserve space to react, or not react at all. You deserve to feel the weight of your love.

Death is the end of someone whom you love, and it is also just the beginning of mourning.

Your life has been permanently altered, but early on your body and your brain haven't even begun to process your grief, yet you push to perform like a normal, fully functioning human being.

You just lost someone you love, and unfortunately this new beginning is the brief period of time when there is a dizzying list of things to tend to in the immediate aftermath of a death. Your capacity for processing said grief is often severely limited during this time, but unfortunately it's also the only time when your grief will likely be fully supported and encouraged by others. The best gift you can give to yourself, or someone who is grieving, is permission to respond however is needed. I coped with my loss the way I cope with most things, by controlling. And I know that I'm not alone in doing so.

Once again, I jumped into action, assessing my various funeral planning spreadsheets and delegating tasks to friends and family members. I honestly have no idea what my father, Sammy, did those few days after my mother died. We were living in the same small house, but I couldn't tell you a single thing he did, and that is okay. If you were the caretaker or are the person in charge of the tons of paperwork that comes with death, it's okay to deal with that as you need to. Alternatively, if you are the person who cannot handle the logistics and just needs to stay in bed and ignore it all, that is also okay. When it comes to grief, especially in the early stages, again, as long as you aren't harming yourself or anyone else, IT IS ALL OKAY. Let your heart guide you through grief.

Grief is never easy, and its form can change over time in the ebbs and flows of life, but giving yourself permission to wholeheartedly experience it makes it more tolerable.

Healing starts when we give ourselves permission to grieve.

2

Safety . . .

When my mom died, I believed I had a role to play, and there was a vision of myself that I didn't feel safe surrendering. I not only didn't know how to be vulnerable, but I equated vulnerability with weakness.

Giving yourself permission to grieve is one thing, but letting it be seen, heard, witnessed even by someone else can be the toughest walk for some of us in our grief journey. How do I say all that I feel? How can I? Who is going to judge me?

Vulnerability has become a bit of a buzzword. Folks on social media get credit for it when they share a picture without makeup on or share that they're having a bad day for any number of reasons. But true vulnerability, the kind of exposure that can feel like an open wound, has nothing to do with social media, or even other people. It is about acknowledging your feelings and expressing them with compassion and care for yourself.

For some people, it's natural: the openness to who they are and what they feel seems to roll out of them like a clear stream; it's respectable, admirable even. For the rest of us, vulnerability often feels like an eternal debate; to share the things we don't even want to admit to ourselves, the secret, and sometimes dark, spots of our mind and heart, the things that we don't even want to feel but can't help feeling—it can seem almost impossible to communicate them to someone else.

As I've considered vulnerability in the context of grief, I've come to realize that vulnerability requires a sense of safety that is not equally distributed in our society. Some people are too busy to be vulnerable. Some of us are too female, too poor, too gay, or too Black for vulnerability—there's no space in our lives for it; vulnerability is something we were not taught, never learned, or had to unlearn given life's challenging circumstances. How do you begin to access the vulnerability that grief requires in the absence of safety and security? If day-to-day living often feels like a battle, grieving seems like a luxury.

When my mom died, I did not feel safe enough, stable enough, to just let go and be truly vulnerable.

I could not afford to fall apart. There was no room to do so and not worry about the consequences. I did not have a nest egg, or trust fund, or backup plan of any kind. If anything, I was the backup plan. I used to tell my mother I planned to be a millionaire by thirty so I could take better care of her. (No this did not happen.) Taking a significant amount of time off from work to focus solely on my grief was simply not financially viable. The idea of centering my emotional needs above all else just didn't seem practical or possible.

In the wake of her death, I also made it my job to take on her leading role as "Strong Black Woman." I was waiting in the wings and prepared to fill her shoes. At the time, I was a Black woman in a very white world; I was Harvard educated and worked on Wall Street, which meant by default almost all of the spaces I entered were full of people who looked nothing like me. I was fresh out of college and the embodiment of the American Dream surrounded by well-intentioned, mostly "color-blind" white people. I was surrounded by wealth I couldn't access. I worked at a bank that had previously held people who looked like me as collateral on its balance sheet. I loved my job, and it provided the means to have health insurance and resources that many others can't afford, but that didn't mean I felt safe. The idea of exposing myself and the fullness of my grief to that world didn't feel like an option. I didn't even feel comfortable wearing my hair in its natural state; there was no way I was going to tell anyone how broken I was by my mother's death. Instead, I went with a version of grief that I thought was more palatable: I started a charity in her honor that the bank supported generously. I told everyone when she died, and they *all* attended her funeral. I spoke openly about breast cancer statistics and the importance of self-exams. I occasionally admitted to my boss Michael that I was sad and let him take me for cocktails and sushi, but that was about as far as I felt I should go with sharing my "feelings." I decided instead to white-knuckle it, and I embraced what Black women have always done: "keep on keeping on." It came to me naturally. The thought of inconveniencing people with my real feelings, feelings I couldn't even admit to myself, the true extent of my pain, was just too much to bear.

The truth is, I was undone. I was a scared kid who'd just lost her mom and had just gotten started in the adult world. If I fell apart, who would care for me now that my mother was gone? Who would even care?

I've come to recognize that we struggle hardest when we don't feel protected. This often makes grief tougher for people of color, Black people in particular, because the safety that vulnerability requires is so much harder to access. How can you grieve when you can't breathe? How can you grieve when you are still forced to argue that your life matters? How can you grieve when you aren't financially secure in a country that lacks a real safety net, a country that has shown time and time again that it doesn't love you? Studies have shown that economic inequity has a direct correlation to mental health. An absence of financial security increases symptoms of depression and anxiety among Black and Latinx people in the United States. So not only have the biased laws, policies, and systems in the U.S. made it challenging for people who look like me to acquire the financial resources that can facilitate proper healing, they have also increased the likelihood that our grief is harder to process because we are more likely to suffer from underlying depression and anxiety.

Because I didn't feel comfortable grieving in public or taking time off to do it, I found hiding places in and around the bank where I worked where I would go to quietly mourn. It was wildly imperfect, but that is often the nature of grief, especially for folks who don't feel like their grief will be honored or supported by others, or who don't have the financial resources to do what they feel they need to do to care for themselves.

Following the death of a loved one, many of us are also often called upon to help support other family members in their grief. When my mother died, neither my father nor my sister asked me to take care of them, but I felt a deep sense of responsibility to do my best to support them both in the absence of the person who had supported us all. During her final years my father and I had shared caretaking duties for my mother. When we knew her death was imminent and she stopped undergoing active treatment for her cancer, I started splitting my time between my apartment in New York City and my parents' home. I handled the logistics: Were her meds organized? When was the next appointment with the pain management specialist? Which lady from church was bringing food on Wednesday? My father managed the heavier pieces, the pieces I simply could not face as my mother's child. He learned how to flush a PICC line, how to wrap her medication ports in Saran wrap so they didn't get wet in the shower. He emptied the portable toilet in their tiny bedroom. He did the things that, in doing them for someone else, serve as an ever-present reminder that whoever the someone else is, is dying.

In the aftermath of my mother's death our combined grief was simply too much for me to bear. At times it felt suffocating. I also felt resentful. I needed my mother, and all I had was a grieving father who, understandably, lacked the capacity to actively parent. My sister was a source of concern for us both. In the years leading up to my mother's death she had been hospitalized for mental breakdowns and suicide attempts on multiple occasions, and she has always struggled during the winter months, so my mother's February passing was especially hard for her. I knew my father and my sister loved me, but I did not believe I could share my grief with them, and if anything, I felt a responsibility to protect them from my pain.

Attempting to quietly return to "normal" life with the worries I carried for my father and my sister, plus my grief, was an impossible mission. My grief had become too much to bear, as I finally came to understand that crying alone in churches and bathrooms during my lunch breaks wasn't working. I was silently carrying grief everywhere with me, and it wasn't manageable. My grief went back and forth to work with me, it was chugging along on the back end of every deadline, whispered to me while in important client meetings, and sat beside me as I laughed along at drinks with my coworkers at happy hours. I was "keeping on," at my own expense. I needed to find a way to own my grief in order to lessen the burden on myself. I could no longer afford to just keep my mouth shut and plow through my pain.

For those of us who have been conditioned to keep our pain to ourselves, moving from a place of silence to a place of vulnerability takes work. You may worry that feeling, really feeling, and communicating the depth of your pain following death will literally break you, that the overload of grief could cause you to fall apart and cease functioning. That it will take you over...plummeting off some sort of imaginary cliff. Many hold it inside because they cannot afford to tumble over; they hold on to the pain quietly like a lifeline, out of a feeling of necessity. Who will catch them if they fall? They think they are surviving. For them, the consequence of getting hit with grief could hurt too bad, land too hard. So they suck it in, hide under water, hold their breath, and swallow more and more of it. And in some form that's what actually wrecks them. It will wreck you too. Shattering occurs when we don't deal with our grief. When we swallow, ignore, or refuse to acknowledge what is begging to be released, we enact violence on ourselves.

The truth is, our feelings only break us when they aren't confronted.

When those feelings are ignored, the violence we are putting upon ourselves is not only emotional and psychological, it can also get physical. Unexpressed emotions increase the likelihood of negative health outcomes. Women are described as the "emotional" gender, but I've found that women, Black women in particular, are very skilled at burying feelings and suffering in silence. Black women have been doing it since we arrived on these shores in 1619. We swallow the pain of racism. We swallow the microaggressions we experience at the office. We swallow the indignity that we feel when white women touch our hair. We swallow the fear and anxiety that comes with being wives, daughters, and mothers to Black men and boys.

The adjectives our society uses to describe Black women are "strong" or "angry," but we are so much more than that. Our experiences in this country and the losses we experience personally are deeply layered. Sharing them should be considered a privilege to those who are fortunate enough to receive them. Yet we swallow, and we strive, and it literally kills us.

Women are skilled at keeping quiet about our pain. This quote attributed to Margaret Atwood encapsulates it all: "Men are afraid women will laugh at them. Women are afraid men will kill them." We carry this fear silently, internally. We grow up knowing that, even if we do all the "right" things, bad things like assault, harassment, rape, murder might still happen to us simply because we are women. We are careful about where we park. We carry our keys prepared to theoretically stab someone—though I have yet to hear if this actually works. We are trained to dress and to speak a certain way and in some professional, community, and even family spaces to simply expect and accept harassment and bear it quietly as though our feelings, our sense of safety, our suffering are all things to be taken lightly.

I knew little about the extent to which my mother suffered physically during her illness because she was so uncomplaining. I often think of my mother's silence. I cannot fathom how horrible it must have been to live with both multiple sclerosis for twelve years and stage 4 breast cancer for three. The one time she did cry out, during a procedure where we would later learn she had not been properly medicated, I stood at the head of her hospital bed and cheered her on like the best doula out there. I held her hand and encouraged her to push through the pain, even though in my gut I sensed something was off, and I was falling apart inside. I watched her cry and writhe in agony while I cried silently alongside her until the procedure was over. When I arrived at the hospital the next day, I was greeted by a social worker who insisted on evaluating me after the trauma of that experience. Months later, I was diagnosed with PTSD.

We are so accustomed to Black women suffering silently that when we finally cry out, speak up, or ask for help, we are often met with disbelief or even minimized by those we love, so we press on. When my mom died, I realized that I was just doing what

I had been raised and trained to do: keep my mouth shut about my pain. I was expected to quietly carry the unattractive, dark, and sad parts of myself. I could talk about my deceased mom performatively for hours at a charity event, but I could not talk about the depth of my pain in any real way. It was too personal, too devastating, and I honestly believed no one would really care.

As Black women, we often try to bury our grief, and by doing so, cause physical, emotional, and psychological harm. I was told by medical professionals that the underlying health condition that created my infertility was likely caused by the stress and trauma I experienced leading up to and surrounding my mother's death. Decades of research have shown that racism and discrimination, in addition to chronic stress and trauma, are linked to a higher incidence of many health conditions, ranging from obesity to breast cancer to metabolomic disorders.

No matter who you are or what you look like, Black, white, Latinx, male, female, trans, poor, working class, undocumented, Jewish, Muslim, atheist, whomever, I'm here to tell you that when you're grieving, vulnerability is no longer a choice; it is a matter of necessity. You cannot neglect your physical or mental health by pretending to be "fine" or "okay." Too many of us have paid a steep-enough price doing that already.

You are worthy of the vulnerability your pain and healing require. Your grief deserves the space it needs. Unburden yourself, put your grief out in the world. If you want to share your pain and don't feel comfortable doing so, ask yourself why.

We give out a lot of cookies for vulnerability these days, and I have come to recognize we give the most cookies to the people who look good being vulnerable. To those who are safe and protected and privileged. It feels nearly impossible to be vulnerable in a world that regularly seeks to silence you or simply ignore your existence. Still, as the writer and feminist Audre Lorde reminds us, your silence will not protect you. It will not keep you safe. So even if you don't feel safe or comfortable being vulnerable and honest sharing what you're feeling, share it anyway.

I learned from not giving myself permission to grieve my mom that I needed to do things differently when, more than a decade later, my husband, Matt, and I lost a much-wanted pregnancy. As I lay on our couch all of those sleepless nights following our loss, I knew that I would not treat this loss the way I had treated the loss of my mother. I had learned too much to let myself simply sit silently with all of these feelings. I would give myself permission to do anything and everything I needed to do to heal.

I had a lot to do to heal and a lot to grieve.

As the classic Black female striver who had actually climbed her way to success and made my family proud by attending a good school, working on Wall Street and in the White House, and marrying a wonderful man, I had convinced myself that I could have and do it all; maybe not all at once, but as long as I worked hard, I would ultimately get what I wanted in life. Why shouldn't I? I did everything in my power to ensure this pregnancy came to pass, I felt I had earned that baby. I felt entitled to that baby. I had a very specific set of plans for myself as a mother. I believed in my bones that I was meant to be a mom. I had worked so hard to bring that life into the world, and then I was left with a failure, and yet another year would pass without my child. I was still physically ill from the miscarriage. We didn't have a backup plan, and I felt lost. It was once again the loss of my identity plus the loss of physical health. It was a grief like no other.

But this time, I told everyone—anyone who would even halfway listen. I immediately posted our embryo transfer photos to Instagram, photos that we had taken to document the day for our child. We'd envisioned these photos would eventually be in our baby book. We documented the whole weekend. Dinner out together the night before in the West Village; walking to St. Patrick's Cathedral the next morning before heading to the fertility clinic. We took multiple selfies and a picture of our embryo, which we had jokingly named Karl. I told everyone on Instagram all about it. I told them how much love I carried for that embryo, and how hard I had worked, and how much of my own body I had sacrificed in an effort to create a new life. I told them I felt like a failure. I didn't do it for their sympathy, or empathy, but because I could not carry the burden of my pain silently again. I gave myself permission to grieve that loss out loud. I would not suffocate this time.

I am not saying in order to grieve fully you need to share your grief on social media. You don't have to do that, but when you keep your pain bottled up and suppressed inside, you are harming yourself, whether the scars are evident today or not. Grief is exhausting on its own, and when you add the work required to cover it up, it's even harder, and will end up mentally, emotionally, and/or physically debilitating in some way. Pain naturally takes energy when it absorbs our bodies and our minds, and it takes effort to convince others we are fine when we aren't. We make grief harder when we fail to let ourselves simply embrace all of its complicated feelings and emotions.

It was personally important to me that I share my pain about my pregnancy loss publicly because I was tired of only seeing stories of infertility, pregnancy loss, and grief from people who don't look like me: white women whom I couldn't fully identify with, given the complexities that come with Black grief. I was never able to just grieve my loss. My grief felt layered with the history of Black women, pregnancy, motherhood, and reproductive health in this country. It was not just about me or "just" about the pain of my pregnancy loss. I carried grief in my bones connected to the complicated history of motherhood and Black women. We are the only beings in the history of this country who have been used both for forced labor and for reproduction. Black women in America have mothered children who aren't their own for hundreds of years. Babies whose mamas were sold downriver. Babies whose mamas got locked up. And lest we forget, the babies we've nurtured and raised on behalf of white women. During slavery, the children we birthed didn't even legally belong to us. My grief was complicated, and I needed to acknowledge that. I had to let myself question what motherhood meant to me, how we defined it as a society, and I had to let my heart break in every direction it took me.

I had to be vulnerable enough to ask the questions, out loud, that didn't have answers. Where does motherhood start? Where does it end? What does it mean to be a Black mother, or to not be one? Is my mother no longer my mother because she's dead? As my mind processed all of this, so did my body. Sharing my full truth became an essential part of my healing process, and remains that way, but it's a continuous journey in giving myself permission to grieve publicly and unapologetically. It does, at times, leave me exposed to people who don't know how to handle it, folks who offer unhelpful comments, opinions, or criticisms. The number of people who asked me if we considered adoption following our pregnancy loss was bananas. Thank you, Captain Obvious; yes, we too have heard of adoption.

When you grieve openly, there is also almost always a crew that will remind you that the terrible thing that happened to you is just a part of "God's plan." Umm, did God call you and tell you all about his plans for my life? Because he hasn't called me, so unless you have access to a valid customer service line for submitting "God complaints," bye Felicia.

I could have stopped sharing, but I refuse to let a few wayward idiots keep me from doing what I need to do to heal. I also understand that other people, especially Black women who have also experienced the same sort of loss, need to know that someone is out there who is going through a similar pain, and that we don't need to hide our hurt, we need to care for it.

Grief is deeply complex, and it isn't something that is meant to be silenced or "managed." It is something that we must regularly reckon with throughout the course of our lives.

Do whatever you need to do to get it out of your body, out of your silence, because your silences truly will not protect you. "They will kill you and say you enjoyed it." Your silence will kill you. And you don't need to add something else to the list of things trying to kill you already. Your pain matters. Your loss matters. And your grief matters. Do not let anyone make you believe that your personal losses don't matter, because they do.

According to every therapist I've ever seen, and specifically grief researcher Dr. Dorothy Hollinger, "To name feelings, to give words—either spoken or written—to emotions that are overwhelming, controls the power of those emotions, harnessing them and lessening their intensity." The simple act of saying out loud, even if it is just to your best friend, what you are feeling in your heart reduces the weight of that feeling. Grief often feels wildly uncomfortable because, like love, it cannot be contained. Do not ignore your grief; name it so it has less power over you.

I recognize that it was easier for me to own and speak up about our pregnancy loss at thirty-six years old than it was to speak about my mom's death at twenty-five; by this time, I was financially well off, and I was running a successful business. I owned my own home. I was married. I had established myself as highly successful by the standards of whiteness and capitalism. If I needed to take some time off work to care for my body or tend to my grief, I didn't feel bad taking it. I knew I was about as safe and secure as one could be as a Black woman in America who isn't named Oprah Winfrey or Michelle Obama. I wish my older self could have gone back in time and convinced my younger self, who did not have all of these things, that she too was worthy of whatever her grief required. No matter where you are in terms of life's circumstances, you are worthy. Your grief is worthy. Your grief is valid no matter how marginalized you may be by society. Do not let anyone else set the standards for who you have to be in order to grieve the way you need to grieve.

The safety that vulnerability requires may not be equally distributed, but we have to find a way to access it in order to live with loss. To arrive at a place with our loss where, at a minimum, we have a handful of spaces, places, or people where we feel safe being vulnerable. You may need that sense of safety in order to tell the truth about the impact of your grief on your life.

Sharing feelings that make us feel ashamed or embarrassed with others is hard. If you can't speak it, write it out. Commit to sharing it, or at least some of it, with at least one other person. Your life, your health, and your heart depend on it.

Our wounds aren't always visible. We are all bruised in ways that the eye cannot see. Pain exists inside, invisible unless we let others know that it's there. Judgment and shame are isolating, and those are the last things you want to do with your grief. Vulnerability means giving something of yourself. It means knocking down walls, barriers, whatever it is you may have surrounding your authentic feelings to keep them unseen. Shame and judgment are often what lead us to hide them; you don't want anyone to ask, "Why are you still so sad?" "Are you still triggered by seeing mothers with their children because of your loss?" Yes, you are, is the answer.

Vulnerability requires you to hand over the truth, especially those truths that you don't want to share. You don't owe anyone anything, but we usually avoid being vulnerable because we fear external feedback. But you have to ask yourself: Is it others who are judging me, or is it myself? People can be assholes, unthoughtful or unkind. Not everyone is going to meet the truth about your grief with empathy and compassion, but you have to remove all judgments, whether self-imposed or from others, and find a safe place to let your feelings out.

And the best person to talk to probably isn't the person you went on two dates with or your office gossip buddy. Given the scope of loss that this country has experienced due to COVID-19, there will almost certainly be someone in your life with whom you can share your full story.

Your grief is yours alone, but you don't have to manage every aspect of grief alone. You cannot do that. Give a voice to what you're feeling. Find the people who value you, and even if it makes you feel weird or uncomfortable, tell them some portion of your truth. Pinpoint the people who respect you and enable them to provide you with the support you need. Grief is nothing to be ashamed of. Grief is love.

3

. . . Feel

GRIEF ISN'T AN emotion that exists solely in the weeks and months after your person's death. **Grief is the repeated experience of learning to live in the midst of a significant loss.** There is no grief time line, because healing is not linear. As you move through your grief and learn to live with your loss, your grief will naturally ebb and flow. And as life progresses, you may experience grief anew quite unexpectedly. Grief is often the hardest in the beginning, and that beginning period can last for months or even years. It can get better and then worse again. And then better again.

This popular concept that there are five stages of grief, and you should be making progress in a linear fashion like following the twelve-step program at AA, is simply incorrect and virtually impossible.

The five stages of grief come from Elisabeth Kübler-Ross's *On Death and Dying*, the book I read in the months before my mother died. What we fail to realize is that Elisabeth Kübler-Ross wrote her famous book for individuals *who were dying themselves*, not for the bereaved. Somewhere along the way, this very important fact got lost in a game of telephone. So not only are those stages of grief—denial, anger, bargaining, depression, and acceptance—not blueprinted for you, even she has said that they are *not* linear. Those stages are not enough to encompass the range of feelings, emotions, and states of being that living with loss, that actively grieving, truly require. This whole idea that you are supposed to go through these "grief stages" in a particular order or else you are "grieving wrong" is simply false. If you have a grief time line or a set of expectations around how you should grieve, write it out, then set it on fire.

Whether it's talking to a dear friend with whom you can be vulnerable with your thoughts, or seeing a therapist, or writing in your journal, in meditation or at a sanctuary, grief needs a space solely for you to spend time with it, to feel it.

Healing is not done in stages, it's done over a lifetime.

Your feelings must not only be acknowledged, but the only path to healing from loss is understanding your pain and sitting with it.

Over the years, I've gotten to know more and more about grief. Grief is having a husband who never knew my mother; Christmases trying to find ways to integrate her into her favorite holiday; Mother's Day in a haze of tears and rosé without my mother or my child. Grief for me is figuring out how to build a life based on the values my mother instilled in me but without any of her actual guidance. It has taken a lot of time and space spent simply feeling my grief to get to a point where I understand it.

As I've mentioned, when my mother passed away, I didn't know what grief was. It was something that people did at funerals, and that was about it. One day a few months after her death, as I stood on the downtown 6 subway platform at Spring Street in Manhattan, I suddenly felt a severe feeling. It wasn't nostalgia, or longing, or even sadness; I now recognize it as despair. I had read of people being suicidal due to loss, but I was used to intellectualizing things, and I knew a little about that from my sister, who had made several attempts as she suffered with bipolar disorder. But I simply could not make sense of all of my feelings. That day all I wanted was a way out of the pain. Those feelings made it hard to simply breathe. With one step off the platform, I could escape the suffering, but as quickly as I considered the idea, I knew that wasn't how my story was meant to end. Somewhere underneath the pain, there was this tiny but powerful insistence that it had to get better. I couldn't feel like this forever. I promised myself that I would find a way to the other side of this feeling, even though I didn't know how. I didn't even know what the other side should look like, but I committed, at that moment, to getting there, to making the space in my life to figure it out.

Living with loss may include times of profound anxiety and depression. Mental illness, suicidal ideation, and thoughts of self-harm are common aspects of the grief experience that no one wants to talk about. Research has shown that the death of a loved one increases the occurrence of several psychiatric disorders, including major depressive episodes, panic disorder, and post-traumatic stress disorder. There is also evidence for increased occurrence of manic episodes, phobias, alcohol use disorders, and generalized anxiety disorder in the aftermath of loss. Because we don't talk about this part of grief, you might feel broken or alone when you encounter these types of struggles in your grief journey. We assume something is wrong with us, but this is all, unfortunately, common.

Grief is unpredictable. It is messy. It is not only emotional but also deeply mental and physical. You may experience some of your worst days and times due to grief. I had insomnia, but then when I did sleep, I'd have dreams about my mom that caused me more grief. I'd wake up screaming or crying. Or there were times I would not cry at all. The only thing that helped me was not letting my grief live on unacknowledged, and lots of therapy.

If you are grieving, lots and lots of people, most people, will suggest therapy or some form of counseling to help you move through your pain, and they are right. But I will not lie to you: finding the right therapist for you is generally a massive, time-consuming pain in the ass. I have had eight different therapists at different points in my life, and one even died when I was still under his care. But therapy helped me in humongous ways to understand my long-term grief. In therapy, I learned that I was terrified of commitment when I met my husband, Matt, because of my grief. I knew what it felt like to love someone with every ounce of my being and then lose them, and by extension, lose elements of myself. My fear of loss was impacting my ability to function comfortably in an adult relationship. My default method for dealing with this fear was flight. I didn't bother fighting, I just put up my boundaries and I'd run away or shut down my relationships. My therapist at the time drew a "boundaries diagram" and assigned me homework. I had to sit down and share with this man I had been dating for maybe nine months that I struggle with boundaries and unconditional love because of my dead mom. I also had to ask for his support and patience. I was mortified. It was truly horrifying, and I cringe just thinking back on it. This man who had never met my mother was now going to have to help me figure out how to move through my grief in the context of our relationship, and we had been dating for less than a year! I had a hard enough time explaining my hair care routine to this white guy from Wisconsin. Having to explain my grief was a whole different level of exposure, but it clearly worked. We've been together for more than a decade, and he can handle my grief, *and* he can give any Black woman who compliments my curls an overview of my care routine.

As painful as it was, the whole process only took four or five therapy sessions, and I was done. Honestly, I didn't even like the therapist very much. She was too close to my own age, and I didn't think she was *that* smart, but she got the job done. Today I couldn't even tell you her name, but she gave me the support I needed at the time.

But I don't want to be another voice in your life pushing you to get therapy.

For some people the idea of therapy is daunting, and I get it. What's most important is that you sit with your feelings and you make time to get to know your grief, as miserable as that may sound.

With grief you have to be like a detective because you never know where it's going to pop up again. A year after my mom passed away, I found myself on a Greek island drinking too much absinthe with a bartender and the morning after I was scrambling to find my lost passport. To some people, it would look like I was just having a moderately reckless good time. Deep down, I knew something else was going on. I had to be honest with myself that the absinthe, Greece, the bartender, it was all just another attempt to distract myself from what I didn't want to do... which was feel. I allowed myself to be the opposite of the controlling, in charge striver that I really am because I believed I needed a break from my life and my grief. I didn't want to sit with my feelings. I honestly didn't want to feel much of anything after my mother was gone.

The idea of just sitting, being present, simply breathing through heavy and challenging emotions seems counterintuitive and, frankly, annoying. Physical pain is, in some ways, easier to manage. I mean, who the hell wants to sit with sadness? With the anguish that comes after a life-changing loss? Who wants to give space to feelings of emptiness and despair? Not me.

But this is what grief asks us to do, to simply create space to feel. The author Glennon Doyle likes to say, "We can do hard things," but when it comes to grief, especially early on, instead of "doing hard things," we need to commit to *being* with hard feelings. We need to be present with all of these hard emotions that arise on and off over and over again as a result of our loss. When I get tired of sitting with my feelings, my friend Lizzie, an actual therapist, always reminds me that the only way to move through painful feelings is to be with them.

Creating space for feelings requires us to move away from the "doing" parts of life. It might mean taking an extra-long shower where you cry hysterically. It could mean spending ten minutes in the morning to journal about your feelings and process just how much you wish your deceased father could be at your wedding to walk you down the aisle. It might mean telling a friend that you're struggling to adjust to a new job in the absence of your partner who has been dead for over a decade. It may just be a few minutes of deep breathing and an acknowledgment that you still miss them. The processing mechanism isn't what matters; what matters is that you allow yourself an opportunity to process the pain and let it take up space in your life.

Allowing ourselves to simply feel difficult emotions is hard because it is counterintuitive, but it really shouldn't be. According to psychologists, at birth we have only six basic emotions: happiness, anger, sadness, fear, surprise, and disgust. Socially, we have been conditioned to believe that most of these emotions are "bad," while others are good. "Bad emotions" are meant to be overcome as quickly as possible. Our culture glorifies the idea of just sucking it up, moving on, and being tough. This is part of what makes living with loss deeply challenging. We exist in a world that tells us that if we feel anything that isn't "positive," it is our job to make ourselves feel good *immediately.* This is a lie. It also just doesn't even make sense when a majority of our six basic emotions, the things we are wired to feel from birth, are, according to our own judgments, "bad." We aren't taught that the best way to get over feeling "bad" is to simply feel. When we let ourselves fully feel these things, without judgment, without even labeling them as "bad," when we create space to process the more difficult emotions that arise in the context of grief, that is how we begin to *feel better.*

It took me thirteen years and a pregnancy loss to acknowledge that one of my primary feelings surrounding my grief is anger—a bone-deep, put-your-fist-through-a-wall type of rage. There is rawness to it. It is well contained, but it burns with the heat that's required to transform metal. I knew I was angry in the days immediately following my mother's death, but I thought I had moved past that, until a somatic trauma therapy session in 2021. I told my therapist, ironically named Lisa, the same name as my mom, that I just felt heavy. I felt worn out by life in a pandemic, by my job, by this book, by my quest to become a mom. Even well-rested, I had this feeling of malaise and exhaustion. As she asked intuitive questions and dug deeper and forced me to really be honest about my feelings and how they were showing up in my body, I realized I was enraged. I am angry that my mom got sick, and I was forced to grow up fast as a result. I am angry over all the pain I had to witness and that she had to experience. I am angry at my father for his inability to fill her shoes after she died. And most of all, I am angry at my mother. I am angry that she left me. I am angry that as a result of her leaving me, she hasn't been around to comfort and console me when my own plans to become a mother were derailed by a rare health condition. I'm mad she wasn't there that day in August when all of the time, money, and energy we poured into trying to become parents came flooding out of my body. I am angry that she isn't here to help me figure out how to navigate all of the scary, weird, and complex feelings I have around her death and my pregnancy loss.

I feel guilty for being angry at a dead person, a dead person who loved me unconditionally. As joyful as I generally seem to be, I realized I was still sitting with all of this anger and resentment toward someone I loved who is no longer here, and the guilt was simply overwhelming. But what I have come to realize is that feelings of anger and resentment don't nullify love; those are the things that make love truly unconditional. Love without conditions means there is space for the ugliest, hardest, most challenging, and most difficult emotions. The people you love the most in life tend to be the ones you are also most often called to forgive. To extend mercy to. Forgiveness doesn't end with death. But that also means difficult emotions don't stop with death either.

I have struggled to accept anger as a part of my grief journey because it somehow feels untoward, inappropriate, and a bit out of control. On some level, I suppose I worried that if I owned up to this rage, I would simply be seen as just another angry Black woman. I couldn't get comfortable with it. And because I couldn't get comfortable with it, I've just let it accumulate in my body and attempted to ignore it, to wish it away. This approach just doesn't work. Acknowledging that anger has played a deep and lasting role in my grief has taken more than a decade and a half dozen different therapists, but now I am claiming it. I am learning to put down the guilt. I know my mother still loves me enough to let me be honest about my feelings of anger and abandonment. I have also learned that anger is a normal part of the grief experience and is especially common for bereaved children. If you feel angry because your mom or dad died, no matter how old you are, that is perfectly normal.

Please learn to own whatever feelings arise connected to your lost loved one. Whether it's anger, frustration, or disappointment, the sooner you own it, the better you will feel. The moment I started to be okay feeling angry is the moment I felt that anger start to shift, to lift, to move out of my body. I felt lightness and ease that had previously eluded me. I think we worry that when we give space to difficult emotions, they will overcome us, when really the opposite is true. Giving space to difficult emotions enables them to move *through* us, not overwhelm us.

I didn't understand any of this in the immediate aftermath of my mother's death, so I made a lot of messes in my early twenties trying to ignore various feelings associated with my grief. I let shame and embarrassment keep me from giving my feelings the space they needed. When I hit the first anniversary of my mother's death, I knew I wasn't okay. The calendar moving from February 28, 2009, to March 1, 2009, likely wasn't going to magically fix me, so I decided I needed to be alone. I needed space to process the truth: my grief hadn't magically disappeared in a year. So I left. I knew my friends and family were worried about me and didn't think this was the best idea, but I stood firm and flew to Miami for a beach weekend alone. It was my first time traveling alone outside of work, and I was scared, but I knew I needed to just feel my feelings from the previous year.

I ran to the water to be alone. I knew it was what I needed to do. In Miami, I found myself surrounded by beauty and had a lovely weekend full of loud, hysterical sobbing in my hotel room and silent crying behind large sunglasses on the beach. It was exactly what I needed, and it was glorious. On my way out of the hotel, when I was headed to the airport, I ran into Seal. I took that as a sign that I'd made the right choice. Running into a gorgeous man who at the time was married to one of the world's most beautiful women must be a good omen. Give your grief the space it needs and do whatever it is you feel will serve as a balm to the open wound created by your loss.

And if you feel weird or uncomfortable or embarrassed about whatever it is you are feeling, remember this: whatever you are feeling is appropriate. Don't limit your definition of "grief feelings" to the obvious choices. The feeling itself isn't what matters. What matters is your commitment to giving space to the feeling and doing whatever you need to process it.

What I've learned most is that instead of fighting

against our feelings, we need to work on letting them take up space. I now allow myself to be overcome by all of my grief emotions, and there continue to be so many of them. It is really annoying. I have way too many grief feelings, but I have stopped trying to intellectualize them and instead I just feel. In giving my feelings, my grief, the space it needs, I have come to the most obvious realization: YOU DON'T GET OVER IT. Whether it's a bundle of cells or a parent, you just don't get over death. You learn how to live with it. We should not think death is something to overcome, because it isn't. We would never expect someone to get over birth; we would expect them to adapt to the demands of parenthood. Why is death any different? The expectation after death should be adaptation as well. You are adapting to life without someone you love. You will make adjustments for your loss for the rest of your life, and this will involve a lot of feelings.

You don't ever "get over" these foundational losses, because the person you lost is core to who you are. They are a part of you. You cannot rid yourself of them, and you never stop sensing, noticing, and sometimes becoming deeply emotional as a result of their life and absence, and that is okay. That is simply part of what it means to be human, and to be loved. Healing from grief, particularly when losses accumulate, requires being honest about what you are feeling, telling the truth about all that you've lost, and letting your heart and your body process that pain. Because the loss was foundational, you will need to get comfortable giving space forever to whatever feelings arise.

It can feel uncomfortable, but that's just a part of the adjustment. At the end of the day, feelings are what they are, and the only guarantee about our feelings is that they aren't permanent. We don't have them forever, and the sooner we accept them, the sooner we learn to breathe through them and feel them, the faster they, in turn, move through us. Fighting painful or distressing emotions, attempting to ignore them, only leads to increased pain and suffering. There is no over, under, or around difficult emotions; the only way past them is through them. So, no matter how inappropriate they seem, our feelings are pure, and they need to be honored. Whether it's laughing at your person's graveside or feeling a deep sense of sadness as your life begins to progress without them, or being enraged over a decade later, whatever it is, it is okay.

And no matter how supportive, or not, your community happens to be, you will still need space for yourself, time spent alone, because your relationship was yours alone, so elements of your grief are also yours alone. People can love on you and support you and encourage you, but they cannot grieve for you.

This is your pain to process, and so much of this work has to be done alone, over and over and over again forever.

Also, please listen to your body. I know it sounds a little woo-woo, but I do believe our bodies sometimes know the things we try to deny, the things we would rather ignore or try to build logic around. In the weeks and months leading up to my mother's death, I knew she was dying, but fundamentally below the surface, there was some denial built in as well. I couldn't bring myself to fully accept just how imminent her death was, so my body reminded me. My relentless anxiety, headaches, and insomnia were all mechanisms my body deployed to help me understand just how serious and how imminent her death was and how hard it was on me. According to Dr. Christy Denckla, a Harvard bereavement researcher, "our emotional states and our bodies are intimately connected... chronic stress can lead to persistently elevated levels of stress hormones including cortisol and adrenaline triggering headaches, migraines, muscle tension, and sleep disturbances." What was happening to me was normal, and I wish I could have accepted it. Your body may be able to help guide some of your decision-making and your emotional processing leading up to and following the death of a loved one.

When I say listen to your body, I mean take a few

minutes, even just two or three, to get quiet and ask yourself: What do you need? What is your body trying to tell you? What are you feeling? What are you physically experiencing that might give you some sense of direction? For instance, if you're someone who always has a nervous stomach before a big work meeting or event, and you suddenly find yourself having a terrible stomachache seemingly out of nowhere, perhaps it is connected in some way to your grief. Or if you are having trouble sleeping and take the time to listen to your body, perhaps you will learn your sleeplessness is anxiety, and maybe some of that anxiety can be worked out in therapy, using medication, or with exercise. Our bodies tell us what we need more often than not; we just need to pause and actually listen to them.

Truly feeling your feelings, being attentive to the hardest and messiest parts of grief, is what makes it easier to live with loss. Entitle yourself to feel whatever grief brings up for you. In many instances, no one else is going to validate your feelings, so you will have to validate them yourself and give yourself whatever you need to process them as they arise and as long as you need to, if that is forever. Giving ourselves time and space to feel and express our feelings is what allows us to move closer to a full and joyful life. Not a life absent of grief, but a life where grief is more manageable.

4

Ask . . .

One night while I was out at the Bryant Park Hotel with work colleagues and clients, everything was fine, and I was having a blast, or so I thought. A few hours into our night out, I was hit with a sudden feeling like an explosion inside of my body. It was an overwhelming amount of anxiety—a panic attack. I don't know who or what triggered it, but I had to get out of there. I felt like I wanted to tear the skin off of my body. I hid in the bathroom and popped a Xanax. When I came out, my colleague and friend Alexa asked me if everything was okay, and because my grief made me a liar back then, I said yes. I downed my dirty martini and left. When I woke up the next morning, I couldn't remember how I got home.

Living with loss requires you to be honest about

the depth of your grief, and to ask for help when you need it. As we've discussed, in this grief journey, we must identify places and/or people where we can be vulnerable and feel safe doing so freely. Being honest about when you need help is also key. Sometimes it might be as simple as admitting that Thanksgiving feels bittersweet because it was your father's favorite holiday, and you don't know how you'll get through making dinner, so you ask your aunt to join you in the preparations. The honesty is about knowing what you need in order to be okay with your grief, with how much you miss your person. It is also about being able to admit at times that you are perhaps struggling with something that feels tough to do on your own. If you refuse to acknowledge your need for help, the need doesn't go away; instead, it will force you to reckon with it, sometimes transforming into acts and behaviors that are reckless.

Mind you, the occasional reckless coping mechanism likely won't cause irreparable harm. I have more than a few ways of ignoring my needs, especially when those needs involve asking others for help. And while I may recommend the occasional stiff drink, or if needed on tough days, a Xanax, I *never* recommend combining the two. I've plowed through numbing my truth using too much booze or boys or benzos, and I survived, but your grief isn't some virtual reality game that you can just escape or run from; it is real, and you need to be honest with yourself and others when it feels too hard to carry it all alone.

When you lose someone you love, some of the people in your life will inevitably try to convince you they are grief experts from the time their dog died in fifth grade. People will quantify your tears: how much, how little, how loud, how quiet, and where did you cry. And, as we discussed, most people aren't honest about their grief because they feel judged. The people who judge you will often be your friends; sometimes they are even your family. They are usually people who love you and are often, rightly, worried about you. At some point, they will inevitably call into question how you are handling your grief. That makes it easier to lie than tell the truth about your need for help. When you aren't "over it" in six months or a year, you feel ashamed. So you don't tell anyone just how bad it really is. You don't tell your roommates you've become afraid of the dark since your mom died and it would help if they could keep the light on at night. You weren't even afraid of the dark as a child, but now you are terrified and anxious at night. You say you fell asleep reading, and that's why the light was left on, but that's just not true. You don't tell them about the vivid dreams you experience that bring both comfort and pain, the dreams where she is there, and you know she is there. You don't tell people these things because you are embarrassed and ashamed. You especially don't tell them because you've been feeling this way for weeks, even years, and you think there's nothing they can do to help.

Then you will have days when you feel better, moments when you feel like your old self again, so you also convince yourself that you are okay, even though you sense that isn't really true. You lie to yourself because you don't want there to be anything wrong with you, and you definitely don't want others thinking there is something wrong with you. Lying about the depth of your grief is like walking on a broken leg. When we lie to ourselves about the weight of our loss, we cause more harm than good. You would never try to walk around on a leg that's badly broken, so why treat your heart any differently?

In February 2014, six years after my mother's death, I still couldn't bring myself to work on her birthday or the anniversary of her passing. At the time, I was working in the White House on a project called My Brother's Keeper. It was an initiative near and dear to President Obama's heart, focused on increasing access to opportunity for boys and young men of color. As a Black woman who spent years in the administration working on racial equity issues,

I was pumped. The energy and sense of optimism around this effort was so palpable you could almost touch it. It was intense and exhilarating, and you could feel it in the air in the days leading up to the public launch of the initiative. We had a date set in February that, thankfully, was neither my mother's birthday nor her death day. Then, a snowstorm hit the nation's capital, and we had to reschedule the event. This launch event involved everyone from President Obama to General Colin Powell and Magic Johnson and a handful of corporate CEOs, mayors, and foundation executives. It was the definition of a Big Fucking Deal in the building, and I was expected to be there as someone who had helped build this thing and had a behind-the-scenes but still very real role to play. Now I was in a full-on state of panic. What if the new date was set for my mom's deathaversary?

I quietly confessed to one of my colleagues, Ari, who happened to be more senior than I was, that if the event was scheduled for February 28, I would not be there. That was my mom's death day; and I love Barack Obama, but I love my mom more. I told him the whole truth, but even six years later, I still cared about what others might think, and I didn't want anyone else to think I was weird, so we agreed to tell everyone else that I had a "family thing" that day. It was a pretty lame excuse, but I wasn't comfortable being honest about my lingering grief. I mean, what kind of Black "family thing" can't be rescheduled for the first Black president, who is trying to launch an initiative to help Black men and boys?

Somehow, by the grace of God and Barack Obama's schedule, the launch was rescheduled for February 27. I worked my ass off and got to be in the room for this historic event. Then I spent the entire next day on the couch drinking bourbon, eating Cheez-Its, and bawling my eyes out. When I told my colleague, Ari, about my "calendar limitations," he said, "Well, if you can't be there on the twenty-eighth, I guess we can't do the event on the twenty-eighth." He did not have enough control to make a decision like that, but he did make me feel better. I only sort of spoke up on behalf of my grief, but I was proud of myself for finding the courage to be honest with even just one person about why I couldn't work on February 28.

The work of grief requires help, and asking for it is not a weakness.

No one else can do the work of healing you, but that does not mean that living with loss is a solo journey. The hyper-independence that we worship is a myth perpetuated by White supremacy and capitalism. The notion that we can or should do things completely on our own was started by a group of white men with slaves and/or servants. What were they really doing on their own? Also, what about the Indigenous people who originally cultivated this land and made it habitable? Weren't they also standing on their backs as well? One of the greatest lessons I learned as a teenager in advanced placement U.S. history is the concept of leisure. You need leisure, free time and space to think, in order to develop new ideas, new theories—like independence, for instance—but we rarely question how that leisure is achieved.

We have been indoctrinated in an ideology of American independence that just isn't true. This country was built by free and indentured labor. And no one does anything truly great without some form of free or paid help. Jeff Bezos built Amazon with an estimated $300,000 loan from his parents. President Barack Obama's career was largely made possible because of a mentor named Valerie Jarrett, his brilliant wife, Michelle Obama, and a group of wealthy Chicagoans who made a big bet. This idea that we have to always do everything on our own is also often rooted in trauma. When you grow accustomed to not being able to rely on parents or siblings or your community for any variety of personal or structural reasons, it makes accepting help more challenging; but accessing help with hard things, whether living with loss or starting a business or becoming a parent, is all perfectly healthy and normal. Somehow we've been taught that needing support—whether emotional support or practical help—means that there is some sort of deficiency within us, and that is just wrong. If you've grown up not being able to depend on others, you grow to believe you must do everything on your own, but it doesn't have to be that way. No one actually does anything that is truly hard completely alone. Whether your support comes from your family, close friends, community, or people you hire, get the help you need in navigating grief. Navigating grief and healing means establishing partnerships, bonds, creating a healing circle of care around you to help you learn how to live with your loss.

The people who love you unconditionally, the friends to whom you can tell the unvarnished truth about your messy feelings, the family members who feel like friends, these folks are essential partners in your grief experience.

One of the last things my mother said to me in the months before she died was, "Always answer the phone for your friends." I never answer my phone, everyone close to me knows that, but what I interpreted her words to mean was, "Show your people you love them by showing up for them." By being there for your people even when it may not be convenient for you, that is an expression of love.

When you show up for your people, the core of your community, no matter what, you also have a right to expect the same from them.

When I was in college, my friend Hamzah once said, "If I never let you inconvenience me, then we aren't really friends. We are just people who hang out and drink together." That very simple statement redefined friendship for me. His statement became the lens through which I evaluated my relationships with those around me. Who was I willing to inconvenience myself for and vice versa? Those are your people—the people who are truly on your team and will show up when things get hard, or when you get hard to be around; the friends who are skilled at rattling off your strengths and weaknesses and love you despite them, or maybe even because of those weaknesses.

And you know what? No matter how much they love you and you love them, they will not fully understand what you're going through, but if they are truly your people, they will want to find a way to help you. If there is something they can help with, tell them.

It took a conversation with my friend's mother, a therapist, to help me identify one of the things I needed in the weeks leading up to my mom's death: a pass. I needed permission to flake on my people. Separate from permission to grieve, which I still wasn't letting myself do, I needed permission to be a shit friend. My moods were unpredictable, my mother's needs were unpredictable as a result of her illnesses, everything in my life felt gray and uncertain, and I needed people to know that I would be largely absent and unreliable. I needed folks to know I was not in a position to be my normal, reliable self. It seemed so simple, but naming that unpredictability via email to some of my friends felt like a huge weight had been lifted off my shoulders. I started the letter like this:

> If you're on this list, by now you've probably heard that my mom is not doing so well. I suppose that is putting it lightly as the most recent update I got from her doctor was six months to a year, and he said "maybe a year" only because she's so "resilient." I am super grateful for all of your calls, emails, invitations to go places, birthday wishes, etc., and am very sorry for not having returned them, but my life has been fairly uneventful from a social perspective and super packed with hospital visits, calls to doctors, fights with doctors, and train rides upstate... Please do keep calling and hold on to those invitations that you have recently extended for dinner, drinks, etc. as I can't really take advantage of them now, but am likely to really need them later.

It was an awkward email to send, but the act of hitting send was immediately met with support, kindness, and love. Although I needed their permission to flake, I asked them to keep reaching out, to set me up on dates, and I asked them to help me raise money for the breast cancer charity I started in my mom's honor.

And I didn't stop there, I kept asking for help.

I had a very specific vision for my mother's funeral, and the funeral programs the church presented to me did not align with that. They were all hideous and so clichéd, with each option some version of "Christian Chic," a sunset or a misty mountaintop or a soaring eagle. I honestly could not handle how ugly they were. I also had a list of brilliant, mostly type-A women who loved my mom, who loved me, and who were ready to do whatever was needed to help me once she died, so I asked my friend Jackie to design simple, elegant, custom funeral programs that didn't suck. I never thought about how they would be printed until I walked into a hotel room where a bunch of my girls were staying and found a full-on print shop. It turns out they had "borrowed" a color printer from Staples with plans to return it the next day. I felt so grateful to have people in my life willing to return a used printer to an office supply store if that was what was required to achieve my vision for my mother's funeral.

And I realized that the help was already there, sometimes without asking; I just needed to accept it.

The days before the funeral I was a mess, and the last thing in the world I wanted to do was go to Sephora, but I needed waterproof makeup. I was not going to have raccoon eyes or smeared foundation at my mother's funeral. My friend Alexa knew it was important to me that if I cried at my mother's funeral, I looked good doing it, so she went out shopping for my makeup. Alexa has blond hair and blue eyes, and I will never know how she figured out the right makeup colors for my milk chocolate skin, but she nailed it.

The toughest part about friendship during loss can be asking friends to help you. It requires you to let them in even deeper than the friendship ever previously required. Grief will present feelings you cannot immediately comprehend. It makes it nearly impossible to convey them to someone else. Asking for help is hard for a lot of deeply personal reasons. Maybe you are used to doing everything for yourself because you grew up in circumstances that required you to be more independent than the average child. Or perhaps asking for help makes you feel too exposed. Fundamentally, asking for help requires us to admit that we can't do everything for ourselves, and that is okay. Let go of any conditioning that makes you feel otherwise.

The fact that you cannot do everything on your own is normal—even when you're not grieving. And if someone wants to help you, but you don't know what you need, feel free to tell them that. If they are your people, and part of your inner circle, they will find a way to make you feel loved even in the absence of your explicit instructions.

When I arrived back in my New York City apartment after burying my mother, I found a stack of cards, a package of fun Hanky Panky underwear, and a blazer from Forever 21 on my bed. Those little treats from neighbors, roommates, and friends did not diminish my grief, but they did make me feel loved and cared for.

When we lost our pregnancy, I was initially in a state of shock and disbelief; I couldn't comprehend what had happened to us, so I was in no position to ask for help or support. I had just returned from buying two of my own pregnancy tests since I didn't believe the doctor's results were correct. After frantically peeing on a stick and seeing with my own two eyes that I was indeed *not* pregnant, I didn't want to talk to anyone, but I knew I needed to tell my crew what had happened. I knew I would need some emotional support. I created a text chain with a few close girlfriends (including a doctor and a shrink), and I knew I could rely on them to share with my other close friends what had happened. I wrote, "I am honestly still in shock, but the test was negative." I didn't answer their calls or respond to any questions. I took half a valium and lay down alone in our bedroom and wept. Matt tried, but there was nothing he could do to bring me comfort in that moment. Three of my friends, not on the text chain but who live locally, descended on our house that night with homemade cookie dough, bourbon, and Chinese food. We watched *American Ninja Warrior*, not a show any of us watch regularly, but a perfect distraction from an unspeakable grief. It was exactly what Matt and I needed that night. I was still effectively high on hormones, existing in a body that believed it was pregnant. I couldn't talk about what happened. I hadn't yet processed it. I hadn't asked for help, but they knew me enough to know I needed their comfort and support, and by showing up they let me know that when I was ready to ask for help, they would be there for me.

No one can replace your person and what they provided you in life. Know that no matter how much your people love you, no matter how much they support you, it will never feel like enough because of all that you've lost. As grateful as I was (and continue to be) for my friends, it was my mother I cried out for. I tend to think of help, particularly in the context of grief, in terms of layers, such as the sand art I loved as a child, with different colors and amounts of sand layered on top of one another. That is how you want to construct your grief support; it's different people, varying degrees of closeness, all of whom are capable of helping you in some way. Some can offer words of encouragement, others can take you out to lunch. Your cubicle buddy at work, whom you sometimes share a bag of chips with. Then there will be people in between—those who will surprise you because of how they show up for you. The neighbor who certainly isn't your best friend but has dropped off a meal. The old friend you haven't seen in years, who stops by to see you the night your mom dies. The distant family member you didn't expect to show up, but who calls weekly to check on you. The strangers who hand you a tissue on the bus or share a kind word, because they understand your loss, some of them instinctively, others because they have experienced it themselves. There is a new intimate bond between you and others. You may not initially realize it, but your loss has recategorized you, and you are now a part of a new community yourself: the grief community.

As you build your sand art, these people who have already experienced what you've experienced can be a critical source of encouragement and support. And while no two losses are the same, it is incredibly helpful to access fellow grievers and make them a part of your team.

I found unexpected kinship among folks I didn't know very well who had lost loved ones. There was a young woman I worked with whose teenage brother had died by suicide when she was younger. When I returned to work after my mother died, she left some of my favorite candy and a mix CD of songs, because it was the 2000s, that she found helpful when moving through her own grief. I used to cry myself to sleep listening to that CD. It was one of the most thoughtful things anyone has ever done for me, and it was totally unexpected. And because she knew grief wasn't just about those two weeks after my mother died, she continued to make me those CDs periodically, without being asked.

Those who know grief will also be a constant source of validation as you live with loss. They are the ones who will know to reach out around your dad's favorite holiday. They will save your dead person's birthday and deathaversary in their calendars because they know, even years later, those dates are still triggering. They will think to ask how you're coping with your grief when something wonderful happens to you. They are your people, even if they aren't your best friends. You are all part of the same shitty club, so you know instinctively how to support one another. They will regularly remind you that your feelings are all perfectly normal.

If you don't have anyone in your life to talk to

about grief from a place of fellowship and experience, consider a community like The Dinner Party, a live or online support group. Being able to commiserate about what it's like to grieve in a world that somehow keeps spinning without your person in it can be very cathartic.

A few months after my mother died, my sister was really struggling to manage her bipolar disorder. It was a devastating and scary time, and I was deeply concerned given her history of suicide attempts and mental health crises. Between my own grief and the anxiety I now carried for my sister, I was something beyond overwhelmed. After I told the guy I shared desk space with at work, Chris, he said, "Your brain can only really be consumed by one thing at a time." He insisted I go to the movies with him and his friends. "A distraction will at least give you a break from all of this," he said. I don't remember what we saw, but it was an invaluable lesson. Sometimes we just need to give our bodies and our brains a break from all of this grief. Chris was never going to be the person I shared the darkest parts of my pain with. Still, even at twenty-four, he was wise enough to know that I was suffering, and he was able to help me get through a really tough few days. Those more casual forms of genuine connection can be a lifeline, especially in the early days, of coping with grief. Sometimes I really needed to be around people who didn't really know how horrific my life was and had been for years. All I wanted was to be "okay." I knew those who loved and knew me most, for instance my roommates Liana and Katie, knew I was definitely *not* okay. Sometimes I felt like I needed a break from their "knowing." One of my other hiding places—in addition to the churches or work stairwells that I mentioned earlier—was at the McNally Jackson bookstore in Soho. I could go there and chat casually with the staff, write, and enjoy a soy latte and a snack without feeling like I was wearing a gigantic sticker that said, "I'm grieving."

Grief support is challenging and complex because the grief we experience is challenging and complex. Grief puts tremendous stress on your relationships. Unfortunately, not every one of my friends stuck around after my mother's passing. It's virtually impossible to be a good friend yourself when you are in the early stages of your grief. You are simply too taxed. You are unable to abide by the normal rules of friendship. Your threshold for bullshit or someone else's feelings is likely momentarily suspended. Your pain has taken over, but then you have good days or even good weeks. You genuinely feel like yourself, and then out of nowhere, something triggers you, and of course the trigger occurs at the most inconvenient time, right when you're supposed to do something for someone else. Just before a dinner commitment you made to a friend for the third time is when your grief shows up and incapacitates you. This is why you need that grief circle, that base of folks who love you unconditionally. I have learned a lot about love through living with loss.

Even when you effectively communicate what you need, set clear boundaries, and ask for help, you might not get it from those you expect to get it from, and you will be faced with another thing to grieve. Relationships you previously treasured can fall apart due to your grief. Friends and family you truly believed had your back, and would always be there for you, will drop the ball. It may not even have anything to do with you, but given the pain you are already experiencing, when someone you believed would show up for you doesn't, it cuts deep. If you have lost a relationship while grieving, know you're not alone. It has happened to most of us, and it's usually both heartbreaking and shocking. In some ways, I've come to simply view it as another aspect of loss that's rarely discussed. It creates a deep wound, but unfortunately it is just another element of the grief experience.

Whether you want it to or not, grief will lay bare who truly has the capacity to love you unconditionally and who doesn't have the capacity to support you for any number of reasons. Grief is a relationship crucible, and just as we cannot control the various feelings that grief presents, we also cannot control how others respond to our feelings and our requests for help. Inevitably someone is going to disappoint you, and some disappointments may simply be beyond repair, while others may be worth revisiting. Only you can determine who is deserving of your grace.

5

. . . Grace

I WAS NOT thinking about extending grace to anyone two days after my mother died. I was standing in my purple-painted childhood bedroom, full of pain and rage. I had just finished basically telling a boy I had just started hanging out with to go fuck himself: "Oh, you heard my mom died, and you didn't know what to say, so you didn't say anything? You know that makes you a terrible human being, right?"

Then Alisha called.

Alisha was my first roommate in college, one of eleven, but the one Harvard randomly assigned me to, whom I shared a small bedroom with for three years, then a slightly bigger bedroom for our last year. Her mother fed me countless meals and washed loads of my laundry. Alisha coordinated my twenty-first birthday surprise with my mother.

Our families, including my grandmother, celebrated Easter together. So I was stunned when I got a call that day and she said, "I have a game. In Portugal."

"So you won't be here for the funeral?"

"No, I'm sorry," she said.

To say that Alisha and my mom were close would be an understatement. She was the person who answered our dorm room phone and consoled my mom when she called, often multiple times when she wasn't feeling well, to remind me of the same thing because the MS was affecting her memory. After college she would call to check in on her, or visit her in the hospital with her favorite dessert, rice pudding. I couldn't believe what Alisha was telling me.

"Okay," I said. And just like that, as I looked out at the gray sky over my parents' backyard, Alisha broke my heart, and I wrote her off for life. "I have a game" sounded to me like the most absurd excuse for not attending my mother's funeral. I was done with her. Though Alisha wasn't playing a random pickup game in Portugal—at the time, she played for the Irish women's national soccer team—I didn't care. I wanted everyone I knew, everyone who loved me and loved my mother, to bear witness to my grief and be present at her funeral. Alisha knew and loved my mom. How dare she not show up for me. She had a deep understanding of just how special and unique my relationship with my mother was because she'd witnessed it since we were eighteen years old. I felt that she should have known how much pain I was in and that I needed her, except I didn't really *need* her. I was surrounded by people who loved me. I had a literal circus of support, but no amount of support was enough, because I had lost my central source of support. I'd lost my compass; I did not need Alisha, I needed my mom.

Alisha attempted to explain her logic. "The funeral is the beginning of grief, and it makes more sense to show up when other people stop showing up." She was right, but at the time I didn't know it. It is hard to let people make mistakes when you are grieving. When someone adds to the deep devastation you're already experiencing, it feels like too much. It may take time, but when people who you know love you don't show up the way you want them to, you have to find a way to tell them and give them a chance to make it right.

I let Alisha know how I felt, and she worked *hard* for years to reestablish trust and to show up for me. She reached out over and over again: letters, emails, care packages, phone calls, offered to run errands or provide practical help to me and my family. When she was in Europe playing soccer, she even sent her boyfriend my way to try to make peace, but I wasn't having it. Eventually, several months after my mom died, she came back to the States and begged (literally) to see me. After much hesitation, I agreed to meet her at Grand Central Terminal for a very brief breakfast before jumping on the train to my father's house. I had planned to help him finish clearing the last bits of my mom's stuff from my childhood home. That day Alisha provided her rationale for why she hadn't been at the funeral, she apologized profusely, and then she jumped on the train with me. It was pretty clear that had been her plan all along, but I was totally caught off guard and was *not* pleased. She literally forced her way back into my life, and as we slept side by side that night in my childhood bedroom, I found it hard not to forgive her. I realized that night that proximity makes hate harder to hold on to. Since then, she has shown up over and over again for me and my grief in a myriad of different ways. If I hadn't been willing to eventually forgive her and extend her the grace that she had rightfully earned, I would have had to add that friendship to the list of things to grieve. If someone really does love you and wants to be a part of your team, they will find a way back in, but only if you're willing to extend them grace and give them a pass. None of us is perfect.

Because people are fallible, they are inevitably going to disappoint you. While you're grieving, someone, probably multiple people, who love you are going to let you down. Given the all-consuming nature of early grief, you are going to let others down as well. You will also have moments when you feel as though you are letting yourself down. When you don't move through key milestones the way you expect yourself to, or when you don't do the things you know you need to do in order to heal. Disappointment is a close friend to grief, and that's why grief requires grace.

Having grown up in the Black church, I can't help but think of grace in biblical terms. I was raised to believe that we humans, as sinners, received the unmerited mercy of God's love and the gifts he chooses to bestow. I view grace as something bigger than forgiveness. Grace is different because it requires forgiveness and some degree of mercy. Grace is a privilege. It is a gift not meant to be distributed lightly. Grace is about giving someone permission to return to a sacred place with you, a vulnerable place. It means once again opening yourself up to being hurt by this person. In the context of relationships, grace is something you earn. It is me making the same or a similar mistake more than once over the course of my ten-year relationship with Matt and not just being forgiven but being let back in fully. Grace means however someone may have wronged you, you aren't holding it against them, you're choosing to let it go. Not everyone is worthy of your grace, and your grief will show you who to extend grace to and who to simply forgive.

Forgiveness is about you, while grace is about other people. Forgiving someone who hurts you when you're grieving does not necessarily mean you let them back in. Forgiveness allows you to let go of the hurt someone has caused you, but it doesn't always mean that you continue to be in a relationship or friendship with that person. You forgive for the sake of helping yourself. You forgive to free yourself from someone else's pain. You choose to let go of the harm that someone caused you because you don't want to carry it. Forgiveness is extending loving-kindness to ourselves by letting go of the hurt. Grace is about extending that loving-kindness to others. Let your grief guide you when deciding which path to choose, but either way, don't hold on to the harm. You're carrying a heavy load already.

Grace is so much more than simply "getting over it" when someone hurts you. Grace is forgiveness plus love. It is the act of welcoming someone back from a mistake and trusting them to do even a tiny bit better next time. Grace is about having enough love for someone, and believing they have the same for you, that you're willing to take a step out on faith. It's about letting them in over and over again no matter what because that's how big the love is, and if you're grieving, that's what you need, and at some point, you need to be able to extend it to others as well.

Grace doesn't mean there are no boundaries or accountability. Boundaries and judgment are important when it comes to whom you decide to extend grace to when you're grieving. Grace belongs with those who do the work to put themselves "back in your good graces." Grace is extended to those willing to acknowledge that *they* made a mistake, and then do the work to show you that you can continue to rely on them, that you can trust them with your pain, with the fullness of your grief.

Extending grace to someone else or to yourself is about acknowledging how imperfect we all are and how complicated grief and life truly are. In the context of grief, there are three ways to think about grace: the grace we extend to others when they don't support us the way we want them to, the grace we require from others as we move through grief and regularly disappoint those around us, and most importantly, the grace we extend to ourselves as we work to rebuild and reimagine our lives after loss.

My mother's death caused me to repeatedly question my aforementioned faith. This idea of grace, whether conveyed by us or by God, was not something I had the capacity to grapple with in the early days of my loss. When you first lose someone you love, your early instincts center almost exclusively around self-preservation. You feel like you might die yourself, so the idea of extending anything to anyone else is beyond comprehension. You have zero capacity, so you focus instead on what you need to do to survive and nothing else. If someone causes you additional pain in those early days, your initial instinct will probably be to cut them out of your life. You just can't deal with any more pain. As you move through your life and start to grapple with the longer-term nature of grief, you realize healing requires you to extend grace to those who love you.

Grief is a lifelong journey, and the folks who support you through your grief are naturally going to require your grace. Oftentimes, when we are grieving, we don't even know what we need, and we leave it to those who love us to guess what we might need from them at any given time. Other times, we might ask for what we need and just not get it from someone we love, because people are human, and humans are fallible. Someone we care about simply may not be in a position to show up for us the way we need them to, and you will have to decide under the circumstances whether or not you extend them grace.

When my roommate Alisha didn't show up to my mother's funeral, I had no idea how much I would need the grace I had initially failed to extend to her. Early grief, in particular, is disorienting and painful in a way that you won't understand until you're there. Those first months and even years are filled with profound instability, which means you are bound to make mistakes with regard to how you treat others and inevitably hurt those you love. Early grief is innately selfish. The brain is consumed by managing the emotional overload of your loss.

Our brain's ability to pay attention, regulate emotion, and complete basic tasks is compromised in the aftermath of the death of someone we love. Simply breathing and inhabiting your own body can feel like a challenge, because it actually is. When you dare attempt to add anything to your plate that is not essential, you frequently fail. Often something totally benign reminds you of the person you lost, and you stop being able to function right when someone else is counting on you. Due to the way our culture treats grief, it feels awkward to express any of this once you're outside of the standard societal grief time line of a few weeks. You may have the best of intentions, but you are often unable to fulfill your ordinary obligations to other people, so you need people to repeatedly extend grace to you, usually without them having any real understanding of what you're experiencing, which is no small task.

In the months and even years following my

mother's death, I could maybe do one thing sort of well each day. This was on my best days. Deep down, I think I knew this, but I couldn't actually admit to myself or others just how incapable I actually felt.

Weekends were my nemesis. On weekdays I could more easily manage because the expectations were clear. They had a rhythm to them. They were structured. Get up, go to work, meet people for drinks, come home, cry, attempt sleep, repeat. Weekends were disorienting. I felt more lost when I was the person who had to figure out what to do with my time. I often felt paralyzed. Work was helpful because it forced me to take a break from dealing with my grief, which is actually just what my brain needed in order to process my loss. Downtime on the weekends was much more challenging to manage because when I was returned to a place without structure, grief literally took over my brain. I didn't have a break from my grief unless I somehow forced it upon myself, to go out, to interact and socialize—and sometimes that just felt too hard. I wanted to move through the world unencumbered and carefree, something I hadn't really been able to do before given my caretaker responsibilities, but I just wasn't capable of it. I wasn't ready.

I was so fragile in those early months and years. I needed people to approach me with kindness, patience, and love. I needed people to extend grace over and over again even though they often didn't know how I was feeling or what I was experiencing because I couldn't find the words to tell them. I was too afraid to tell the truth. All of these deep and heavy emotions overwhelmed me, and I know it couldn't have been easy being a friend to me in those early days.

When I am struggling, I also often find myself unable to be a friend to myself as well. Years later, as we moved through our infertility journey and subsequent pregnancy loss, I struggled to treat myself with the grace and care I needed and deserved. In 2017 we believed we were finally going to become parents. We found our egg donor and got to work creating embryos we believed would turn into our children, or at least one child. As we watched every single one of those early embryos fail for one reason or another, we experienced an extended period of hope followed by brokenheartedness. With six eggs, we were confident at least one would work out and become our baby. Still, over the span of a few weeks, as we held tightly to our hope, we experienced failure after failure. In this moment of grief, I learned how much I really wanted to be a mother and how much of our parenthood journey really was outside of our control.

As our friends began to get pregnant and have

children, we committed to holding joy in our hearts for every new announcement, for each baby who would call us Uncle Matt and Aunt Marisa, at times failing to extend grace to ourselves. During our first pregnancy attempt, after our final embryo failed to make it, we were scheduled to attend a baby shower for Matt's childhood best friend, Scott, and his wife, Megan. Megan insisted that we did not have to attend the shower. She offered us a pass, and I didn't take it. I love Scott and Megan, and I felt being around Scott would help facilitate Matt's healing process, but I didn't consider my own healing. I failed to prioritize my pain and extend myself the grace I needed in that moment, the grace that Megan offered. I thought I would be fine. I told myself, "This isn't like when your mom died," and it wasn't, but it was still grief. I needed to stay home, but instead of honoring my needs and extending myself some grace, I told myself to suck it up and silently cried myself to sleep every night we were there.

I wanted to celebrate Scott and Megan and this baby girl, whom I already loved, but I should have done it from afar. I was angry that being around someone I love who was having a baby made me sad, so I tried to deny those feelings. I just didn't want to deal with my grief. As per usual, it felt like a massive inconvenience, so I just tried to push through, which was a mistake. Grief requires kindness, flexibility, and a near-constant reevaluation of your needs and expectations in order to properly heal.

If you are able to extend grace to yourself to see yourself as the imperfect human that you are, full of the complicated feelings that accompany a loss, feelings that ebb and flow, you will be more able to extend it to others as well. When we refuse to offer ourselves grace and accept whatever we are experiencing, we make it harder to move through it, *and* we make it nearly impossible for others to effectively help us.

Grief is a tricky beast, and there is no such thing as grieving "perfectly." Be prepared to extend grace to those around you, but most importantly, you need to extend grace to yourself.

6

Intimacy . . .

I MET MY husband, Matt, four years after my mother died. I quickly learned that finding your way back to unconditional love after grief is akin to finding your way out of a house of mirrors at a carnival. It is dizzying, overwhelming, and to maintain an intimate relationship or build a new one is unfathomable. When you've loved someone fully and let them love you back, and then they died, subconsciously you're reminded about death when it comes to love, more than life. I found myself waiting for the other shoe to drop. Who might die next? My dad, my godmother, my grandparents, who knew. Sometimes it seems easier to just walk away from ever loving someone again than to expose yourself to the possibility of that type of grief ever again. But that's impossible. I couldn't stop loving my family, and I couldn't stop myself from falling in love with Matt. The depth and the ordinariness of grief are most obvious when you realize that you love someone new.

I knew early on that Matt was worth whatever fear I needed to manage in order to be in a healthy relationship with him, and as I mentioned, I went to therapy to accomplish that. Matt and I met on the dating site eHarmony. On an otherwise unremarkable weeknight, I found myself on a date on a blustery evening in January with a guy from Green Bay, Wisconsin. I learned within about twenty minutes that he had been married before, was a die-hard Packers fan, and was missing half of one of his fingers. I was definitely intrigued. At the time, I was working for President Obama, owned my apartment, and thought I'd finally succeeded in fully "getting over" the loss of my mom. I felt fine, and then this guy showed up. Our relationship was new, exciting, and life-changing, and therefore brought up new and uncomfortable feelings of grief.

With the help of therapy, this new wave of grief subsided, and I realized the work of grief and learning to love again after loss is never-ending. My new commitment to Matt was emotionally triggering for me over and over again.

One day after I'd sort of figured out how to

be an adult in a loving relationship with another adult, after many good days spent watching Packers games, eating too much food, or going for hikes in the D.C. area, Matt and I got into one of our first, and worst, fights. It was over something so small, I don't remember what it was, but I just wanted to get away from this man. I wanted to, but I had nowhere to go in the 650-square-foot studio we shared. I had just finished cooking dinner, so I just stuck my head in the refrigerator. I was pretending to look for something, but really I was just hiding and trying to control my rage. After maybe forty-five seconds, Matt asked, "Are you just going to hang out in the refrigerator all night?" This was obviously an appropriate response to my childish behavior, and we both started cracking up. I knew my mom would have laughed at that story and probably taken Matt's side. At that moment, I instantly felt her absence. Not having her around to share all of the random and unfamiliar and funny things that naturally arose at the outset of our relationship was hard. As much as I knew that Matt was the guy I would end up marrying, especially after we adopted our dog Sadie, it was tough to swallow that I couldn't share that with my mom.

Expect that maintaining or building any intimate relationship after your loss requires some degree of shared grieving. As our relationship continued to grow, Matt was repeatedly called to grieve alongside me; he became my Grief Partner. This does not mean that he had to be sad when I was sad. A Grief Partner isn't about sadness as much as it is about support. It means that if it's your mom's sixtieth birthday, and she has been gone for eleven years, your Grief Partner will help you do whatever you decide you want to do to acknowledge the day. You need your Grief Partner to be nonjudgmental and actively supportive. If I decide to throw a party for my mom's birthday, Matt buys the candles for the cake. It is hard to grieve someone you never knew, so I don't expect him to share all of my feelings, but I do request and expect that he meet them with empathy, understanding, and love.

Together we've navigated the loss of my mother and devised ways to include her in our lives, from our annual holiday party, "Tacos and Baby Jesus," to our outsize Easter celebrations, to my monthly roast chicken. On the anniversary of her death, Matt takes off from work as well, and we do something, sometimes even just watch TV, as a family. I felt like we had nailed grief as husband and wife, and Matt had nailed grief support, until our pregnancy loss. This was the first time that we grieved the same loss together as a couple. A single day in August completely upended my understanding of grief, love, and marriage.

Our grief story changed when I found myself curled up on our bath mat that fateful late summer day. I realized then that grief isn't just a single event. There, on the tiled floor, I experienced a new grief. A new pain. This grief came with a horrible physical pain: I experienced severe bodily symptoms and hormonal withdrawal, followed by intense anxiety and depression. My grief was delayed by all the medical procedures that come with a miscarriage. There was a laundry list of doctor's appointments, blood tests, and physical exams to get my health back on track and maybe get me pregnant. It was too much to bear so I mostly returned to my usual bad habits to cope, making lists, doing research, burying myself in my work, and subjugating my emotions.

While I spoke to doctors and tried to figure out if I could get pregnant again, Matt actively grieved our loss. He let his heart break and allowed his mind to be consumed by sadness over what could have been. He worked to process his emotional pain, which put the two of us in very different places. I hadn't even begun to grieve when he reached a point where he felt he had processed the loss and was ready to figure out our next steps as a family. All I could think was, are you serious? How could he be talking about things like surrogacy and adoption while I was still bleeding for no apparent reason?

Grief experienced in intimate relationships and marriages is complicated. There was no escape from the pain and brokenness for either of us. He couldn't ignore my sadness, depression, and anxiety when they finally fully arrived, and I couldn't keep my envy at bay when he didn't share these emotions. Our ability to support each other was limited. We each processed the experience differently, needed different things, and at different times. I began to see how loss can break an otherwise stable relationship.

Managing shared loss in an intimate partnership is deeply complex, and wildly uncomfortable, and at times everything will seem upside down. The relationship you've both normalized is pushed aside when you're dealing with grief. Grief impacts how you react to the world mentally and physically, and that doesn't stop with your relationship. Grief is all-consuming and requires your attention. Whether you are grieving the same thing or something you experienced separately, when grief enters the relationship, it can be lonely. You are different human beings, and either one or both of you are going through an intense period. There are plenty of opportunities for resentment to fester and frustration to produce fissures too deep to mend.

Matt and I had to recognize that there were limits to how much of our grief we could share.

We were each over capacity on our own and had very little left to offer each other, and we had to be honest about that. In theory, we maintained tons of empathy and gratitude for each other, but, practically, we were severely limited and often became irritated with one another.

The best thing you can do in a relationship, in any challenging situation, is be honest. Without shame acknowledge what you can and, more importantly, what you cannot provide, and encourage your partner to do the same. When we were four months out from the pregnancy loss, I told Matt that I felt his patience with me had grown thin. It was the holiday season, and I didn't have any of my usual excitement. I even wanted to cancel our aforementioned taco party, which pays homage to my mother. I just couldn't do it. I was still dealing with physical side effects and lingering depression while he seemed to have "moved on." He admitted that he hadn't moved on, but he'd decided how he wanted to deal with our loss and grow our family. He acknowledged that he was struggling to be sensitive toward me, and he honestly didn't understand why I was still so sad. Just having him admit that we were in different places and that his capacity was limited was validating. It reduced my resentment that we were in different places. He also got the freedom to admit how he was feeling and how it differed from how I was feeling. Neither of us knew what to do about it. We just realized that we were grieving together, but we also needed to grieve apart. I had to access my own coping mechanisms, which were often not the same as his. We both needed to do it unapologetically. I had to tend to my grief and needed to make space for it. We each had our own therapist. We have our own circle of supportive friends, and respected that. We became more mindful of what helps us individually live with the grief. For Matt, it could be zoning out playing a video game, whereas I'd journal. And sometimes we could mindfully support each other through exercise, meditation, and laughter when times got hard. Most importantly, we've learned to be unwavering in our support for each other when it comes to creating the space to do the things that help.

Though we took those helpful actions, anyone in an intimate relationship knows that you enter a room in one conversation and can leave in a very different one. With this in mind, Matt and I set time lines around discussing our grief with each other. I've found that this helps in terms of having a Grief Partner but also in growing our relationship. If you are living in the same place, grief can be a lot to unload on someone regularly. Instead of sharing daily, perhaps you set aside a specific time to discuss what you're each experiencing once a week if you're both grieving, or the type of support you need if only one of you is. Grieving with someone else or while being in a relationship requires clear boundaries. Research has shown that holding back grief to not overburden your partner actually has the opposite effect. When you are in a deep partnership with someone, you can tell when they are off and/or not being totally honest. Don't let your grief push you to lie to your partner about how you're feeling. Because Matt felt better than I did, sometimes he wanted to spend time with people or do things that I just wasn't up to doing. A few days after our loss, one of our friends was hosting a pool party. Everyone would be there with their children. There was no fucking way I was going. Matt, on the other hand, clearly needed the distraction, and I was happy to be on the couch by myself watching TV, so I encouraged him to go without me. I never wanted him to feel guilty for leaving me at home, so we just had to be very clear with each other about what we wanted over and over again until we were back in a similar place emotionally.

Fundamentally, grieving while in an intimate relationship with someone requires you to constantly assess what you need, find a way to share it, listen with empathy to what they need, and lovingly find a way to navigate your shared pain in different ways.

Mutual respect and a shared commitment to healing is critical when you've experienced a loss together. Though we decided to tell the truth about what we had experienced, I am more verbal than Matt. In communicating, it helped that we were aligned on not keeping our infertility and resulting pregnancy loss a secret. And we wouldn't tiptoe around each other like it didn't happen either. We do not do secrets in this family. It may have only been a bundle of cells, but it was our bundle of cells. We named those cells. We had hope for those cells and our future as a family. We loved that little bundle of cells, and because of that, we expect to reflect upon what happened, and at times grieve together and separately for what might have been, for the rest of our lives.

We both knew that grieving together meant that we needed external support. He could not be my Grief Partner while grieving himself, and I couldn't be that for him. We needed the other people who loved us. Friends showed up with chocolate, wine, or home-cooked meals. Friends and family from afar checked in on us regularly, and we embraced it, separately and together. Some days I really needed to catch up with a girlfriend, and if Matt didn't feel like company, he left the house and headed to the driving range. We committed to accepting what each of us needed, even in the realm of external support. Other women and men who experienced the painful sting of pregnancy loss and infertility became a source of ongoing support for us as well. If not for all of the external love we received, our pain might have suffocated us and harmed our marriage. I recall thinking to myself on more than one occasion, "I understand how things like this can lead to the end of a relationship." Navigating the searing pain of loss with your partner tests the strength of your marriage and your capacity for empathy.

And no matter how committed you are or how strong your marriage is, at some point when navigating loss together, you will both fuck up. You will fail to show up for the person you love, and they will fail to show up for you. You are too focused on surviving this horrible thing, and you will drop the ball, and it will suck. You will feel horrible hurting them, and you will have to regularly extend grace to yourself and your partner and ask for it from them in return.

Whether you're making your way back to unconditional love after a loss or navigating loss with your partner, you are taking a risk: the risk that this other person won't be able to effectively hold space for your grief. The risk that grief will break your partnership. The risk that at some point, one of you will be the ultimate cause of grief to the other. But you have to take the risk. You are still here, but you're not "living" with loss if you're constantly living in fear *of* loss. Whether you're bringing your own grief to the table or sharing a loss with a partner, take the risk. Don't let the potential, or eventual, cost of unconditional love keep you from sharing it with someone else.

7

. . . Care

It is counterintuitive for many of us, but after we lose someone we love, we have to figure out what kind of care we need in order to live with loss. We must figure out how to rebuild that pillar of care and support that they provided within ourselves after they die.

Often, the choice to care for ourselves is one riddled with guilt. No one teaches us as children that taking proper care of ourselves is part of living a full life. Self-care is essential to healing not only physical but also emotional wounds. Taking good care of ourselves is a part of what we all need to do to simply function as human beings. And it becomes non-negotiable when you are grieving. In grief, we must identify the ways in which the person we lost cared for us and apply that care to ourselves. It will never be perfect or seamless because, at the end of the day, all we want is for that person to take care of us, but it is truly the only choice we have. When I find myself longing for my mother, when all I want is to put my head in her lap and have her rub my back and tell me everything will be okay, I have to ask myself: What is it that I'm truly longing for? Is it comfort, consolation, a loving touch? I let the answer guide me toward what I can provide for myself. Whether it's having a conversation with my husband or girlfriend that I need, a visit with my therapist, a massage, whatever it is, I give myself permission to access it because care is essential to healing.

It can be hard, especially when we are accustomed to being caretakers for others, to care for ourselves. Everyone says to put on your oxygen mask before assisting others, but how do you do that when you have children, a business, or other responsibilities? But the care I'm asking you to dive into isn't about a mani-pedi on the weekends or a gym membership. Sometimes caring for ourselves isn't about saying yes to a wellness treatment, but about saying no.

In November of 2019, three months after our pregnancy loss, I decided I needed to put myself and my care first. As I crawled off an examination table and onto the floor in an empty gynecologist's office, I told myself, "I can't keep doing this. I'm just not strong enough." That is the moment I realized I had hit rock bottom in my pregnancy journey. I needed to stop trying to become pregnant and focus on myself. Months after our loss, I was still physically ill. I was at my doctor's office having tests run, blood drawn, and enduring another invasive examination. Physical exams had become a near weekly occurrence, and I was having more vaginal ultrasounds than I could count—sometimes every few days. After several weeks of heavy and unexplained bleeding, I begged a nurse to fit me in with an on-call doctor at my gynecologist's office. They squeezed me in during the lunch hour. Following a brief and painful physical exam, the doctor admitted he couldn't definitively identify the source of my bleeding, so to be safe, he needed to test me for uterine cancer. *Could I really have cancer after enduring all this other shit?* I thought. That would be too cruel. Given all the physical and mental suffering I had recently experienced, it couldn't possibly be that bad.

They proceeded with an unmedicated endometrial biopsy to be safe. I knew it would be super painful when the nurse offered me her hand to hold. It was much worse than anything I could fathom. They dilated my cervix, ironically what happens naturally at the beginning of labor, and then suctioned samples from my uterus out of my body as I lay on the table, attempting to breathe and distract myself by digging my nails into my own hand.

Following the procedure, the doctors and nurses left, and I was alone. I wanted to throw up or pass out, but I just lay there on the table, bleeding and sobbing silently. I didn't know exactly what would come next on our path to parenthood. I knew there would be more tears, frustration, and disappointment for sure, but as I crawled off that examination table and onto the floor, I made a firm decision. There would be no more attempts at pregnancy for me. No more fertility treatments. No more being poked and prodded on a near-daily basis. No more praying for a positive pregnancy test. Pregnancy was officially off the table for me. I just couldn't do it. It was time to take a break from trying to become a mother and instead focus on mothering myself.

I needed to embrace self-care, a concept I had always struggled with. I needed to do what Black women have been doing for others for years: I became a caretaker again, but this time I became one for myself.

The moment I said no to my dream of pregnancy and motherhood and yes to caring for myself was not a moment of peaceful acceptance. I was embarrassed by my decision, uncomfortable with what felt like a selfish choice, and once again I felt like a loser. I hated myself for it. Why couldn't I just keep moving forward? Pressing pause on my dream of motherhood, on this thing I had desired and worked to accomplish for years, to take care of myself, felt weak and pitiful. I felt guilty for my inability to continue to sacrifice my mind and body for this child that Matt and I so desperately wanted.

Choosing yourself and the care you need feels selfish and, at times, irrational, especially if it comes at the expense of a long-held dream. If you lost your spouse three months ago and choose to prioritize your care over the big promotion you were just offered, it might feel counterintuitive or just plain wrong, but it's not wrong; it's just not what we are used to. Like most of us, I wasn't raised to prioritize caring for myself, and when I did "care" for myself, it was usually in superficial or indulgent ways. I would buy a new dress or get my hair done, but nothing deeper or more intentional or thoughtful.

There is this standard playbook for self-care sold by social media influencers and motivational "experts," but care is really all about you and what you need in order to love and take care of your inner self. It means caring enough about yourself to take the time to access the things that make you feel whole. What you need to be your version of complete. There will always be a sense of absence, a piece missing, a longing for what you've lost, but there is also a pathway to wholeness, but only if you give yourself the care that you need.

Following both of my losses, I simply needed time. I needed time away from work and from other people in order to process what I had experienced. I needed to write. Writing is often how I get at what I am actually feeling. And I am not talking about writing this book or an article for *Vogue*; I am talking about writing for the sake of processing. I needed to see on paper what had happened to me. I write to get things out of my head. I write to obtain clarity and to unburden myself. I write to make commitments to myself. I needed to write over and over and over again, "I am meant to be a mother." In the face of my loss, I needed to remind myself of what I already knew in my bones. I didn't know what the path forward was going to look like, so I needed to remind myself of the ultimate destination.

With the addition of therapy, this helped me move through our loss and served to fortify me for the work that grief requires. Still, ultimately there is an element to care after loss that is deeper than simply accessing the "things" that help us heal.

The truth is, you can do all of the right things and still not feel whole. For the most part, I knew "how to do grief" after my pregnancy loss, but when I'd check in with myself, I didn't feel like it was helping. I felt like a big fucking mess. I was still challenged to live my daily life, my grief blanketed everything, and I didn't know what to do. My new loss challenged my assumptions of what I knew about loss. I thought that I could rely on the muscle memory of grief to get me through this loss. Many people will say, "I've already been through the worst," or "I've been here before," but that's not how grief or healing works. You can't create a program around your pain or healing. Each new loss has a rhythm of its own. There are different waves and challenges for every occurrence in your life where you experience grief—whether it's through death or some other kind of loss, a breakup or friendship ending, losing a job. Any kind of loss introduces a new set of feelings and new requirements for your healing. Every new loss also has something to teach us, whether we like it or not. My pregnancy loss taught me that effort does not always align with outcome. I poured everything I had into getting pregnant—I literally let someone electrocute my fucking uterus—and it just didn't work.

I also learned that I needed to finally mother myself. I needed to treat myself with the gentleness, kindness, compassion, and love that my mother always had for me. This was a major step toward healing. I worked to identify all that there was to mourn, and I mourned. I cried constantly, and I was honest about what I was feeling. When friends visited from out of town with kids, I told them I didn't want to spend my day with their kids. It was too triggering at the time. I honored the boundaries I knew I needed, even when it was uncomfortable.

You are worthy of all the care that you require in order to heal from your loss. And why wouldn't you be? You were worthy of the love you shared with your person, so you are worthy of the love and self-care that your healing requires now that they are gone. Self-care requires you to treat yourself the way you would treat your best friend, or your sibling, or your spouse. It means saying no if someone from work tries to schedule a meeting during your already scheduled therapy appointment or much-needed workout. It also means saying no to people who don't respect the boundaries you require right now.

Self-care can be counterintuitive. It can be a struggle to release yourself of the mindset that you can do it all, that you don't need a reset or even that much healing. It can sometimes require some assistance to get you there, to a place where you learn to prioritize this area of your life in general, but especially while grieving a loss. Many of us struggle to be kind to ourselves, and this is especially true when we are grieving. It is particularly difficult for those of us who are built to love and nurture others. My mother hadn't just been my mother; since I was thirteen she had also been someone I cared for, someone at times I was responsible for. When this is the case, we have a hard time learning how to care for ourselves. It is different, and it requires practice. Often we wait and hope for others to provide us with what we need, and when they fail to, it hurts. Real, non-Instagram-worthy self-care requires you to love yourself more and more every day. To see yourself as a person of value and worth. To believe that needing care doesn't make you weak. It makes you human. In society, women especially are raised to give their love away to others—our children, spouses, communities. But in order to do that effectively, we have to give it to ourselves first. When I am in a place where I feel overwhelmed by my responsibilities to others, sometimes I can have a conversation with myself and remind myself to take a quiet moment to think about what I need.

Life lived during a pandemic with a spouse working on the front lines was stressful and isolating. I often had to just sit down, get quiet, and ask myself, "What do I need? What might make things a little bit easier?" Other times, especially if I've really dropped the ball on caring for myself in the midst of a busy professional season, I have to call in reinforcements. I'll ask my friends Allison or Adriana if I'm going too far—should I take on another client, or a new project, or go somewhere and sit down and relax? These ladies force me to be better, kinder, and less judgmental of myself. When we haven't been trained to take care of ourselves, it helps to be able to ask for help. Caring for myself is one of the ways I know I can make my mother proud. It's how I show her that I really am okay even though she isn't here.

After I decided I would no longer try to get pregnant, I thought I was fixed. I thought my grief would end and I would be okay. At first, I didn't slow down; I pressed on with work and life and friends, I thought I could just "keep on keeping on," and then the entire world slowed down. It was the pandemic. I canceled a much-needed beach vacation in March of 2020 and asked my husband, a public health expert and scientist, if he thought we would be able to just shift the trip to August. The look on his face was enough to tell me I had no idea what was coming. As we were all confined to our homes, cut off from family and friends, and stripped of any sense of normalcy or routine, we grieved collectively. Surrounded by death and disease as COVID-19 ravaged our country and the world, I mourned my personal loss and the losses we all experienced together. The early days were a struggle. The little things that often helped me get through my personal grief were no longer accessible. We didn't feel safe ordering our favorite Mexican food or leaving the house to meet an always cheerful friend for lunch, and in-person church and therapy were both off-limits. Small luxuries that previously helped prop me up during difficult times were taken away during an incredibly challenging time. I feared I would never see my elderly grandparents alive again, and then the person whom I never thought to worry about, my cousin Ebonee, died from COVID-19 at thirty-five. Having to call my mother's little sister and review COVID protocols for a small, masked outdoor memorial service that I wouldn't be able to attend was horrific. All of the isolation and grief forced me to be by myself and led me to deeply and intentionally process my pain and truly take care of myself, and it was not easy.

Self-care can be a blurry place to navigate under normal circumstances, and it is especially tricky when you're grieving. It may look fun to people on Instagram with #SelfcareSunday, but self-care in the context of grief requires a serious deep dive that goes beyond a day at the spa. You have to stop reaching for distractions and listen to your heart, and there is a deep need that sits beneath all of the pain, longing, and sadness. What is it that *you* really need? What does your grief require? There is something specific and internal that your heart is calling for that only you can answer. Do you need to forgive that sibling for abandoning you when your mom was sick? Do you need to forgive yourself for not being there when your dad died? Do you need to give yourself permission to envision a new future without your spouse of twenty years? Do you need to do the work to accept that your stepfather has started dating just months after your mother's death? Do you think your miscarriage was your fault? There is always something internal that you must resolve in order to access the strength that living with loss requires. You can't turn away from it or ignore it. It will follow you, and only you can determine that deep need and the healing it requires. Many people, myself included, find it helpful to journal, exercise, or meditate, but it's really whatever helps you quiet the inner voice that is running through your to-do list from work and create space for your soul to speak. Life isn't about your to-do list or achievements; it's about caring for those unseen parts of you. When you take the time to get to know those aspects of your heart and spirit, when you determine what it is you truly need, you can live a full life in the midst of your grief. It's where healing can be most active and the well from which joy and love can flow.

In my journey, I've realized that my struggle with self-care, with choosing to prioritize my needs above all others, was likely connected to some internalized multigenerational trauma. As a Black woman I have always felt most comfortable striving. Proving my self-worth by racking up accomplishments and succeeding professionally has always been my jam. I've come to see that part of why Black women are often described as strong is because we have no choice but to be strong. From childhood onward, we are trained to protect ourselves. Our forms of "self-care" usually arrive in adolescence or earlier, in the form of things that will help us fit in, like relaxing our hair, and get by in a country that has only ever affirmed our worth at slave auctions. We are raised from a young age to be tough and uncomplaining, because that is what society requires. If you ask my father's ninety-eight-year-old mother how she is feeling, she will generally say, "I feel all right. Ain't no use complaining anyway cause don't nobody want to hear it." At her age she's survived numerous heart attacks, strokes, quadruple bypass surgery, and casual and violent racism and sexism, and she watched her daughter-in-law, a woman she knew and loved as one of her own for over thirty years, die. Personally, I think any complaints she has are pretty valid. Black women are taught to move through this country not only bearing the regular indignities and slights that come with preconceived notions of Black women, but also the scars of our history. I move through the world as my ancestors' legacy carrying the trauma and pain of racism, carrying all they were forced to overcome and endure, and also the pressure to make it because of all they have been through. You are not expected to seek rest or care beyond the care you put into your appearance as you strive to be "twice as good." I don't even think my grandmother believes my job is hard since at least I get to work indoors. As mothers, 67 percent of Black women are the primary breadwinner in their household, and on average, Black women only earn sixty-two cents for every dollar a white man is paid. If we didn't strive and succeed and regularly "make a way out of no way," entire families and communities would be harmed. How can we create room for self-care under these circumstances?

Striving had always been my answer to trauma. I took care of myself by literally taking care of myself and ensuring that the "bad" things that happened to me didn't get in the way of my success, and I just couldn't do it anymore. Research has shown that multiple, compounded traumas are harder to cope with and linked with a higher risk for physical and mental health problems. I needed a fucking break.

All the therapy and Peloton rides in the world were not going to save me if I couldn't stop and really, deeply, thoughtfully care for myself. It was hard to acknowledge that I needed to stop trying to become a mother and spend some time mothering myself if I ever wanted to reach a place of true wholeness. I wanted my mother there to do it for me, but that just wasn't possible, so instead I had to ask myself: What would she say? What would she do if she were here? How would she help me? And then I had to do those things for myself.

I know she would have told me to rest, to take a break, to go to the beach, to stop being so hard on myself, to be patient with my body, and treat myself with love and kindness and compassion. As I considered what she would tell me to do and then actually did it, I began to realize that after her death, *I needed to rebuild that pillar of love and support that she provided.* No one can replace your person, no one can be your mother, father, brother, child, or friend again after their death, and that absence will be there forever, so you have to ask what that pillar of support provided for you. This is what you're listening for within yourself. If your dad was your biggest cheerleader, get cheering. If your wife was the one who provided positive words of comfort during difficult times, start writing out some affirmations for when things get hard. Your person was in your life to teach you these things. The love and support they provided you with through their smiles, the comfort you received when they held your hand, their encouraging words, or just being themselves in the world with you—we cannot replace that with new people, but we've learned what it's like. We can access what they provided by going deep within ourselves to find what they taught us.

And as I mothered myself, I took the time to process all that I'd lost and learned over the last twelve years and a lifetime with my mother. It was a daily act figuring out for myself how to make sense of it all and how to move forward. The pregnancy loss reinforced for me that these foundational losses are core to who you are. They are a part of you. You cannot get rid of them, and you never stop sensing, noticing, and feeling their presence. It's simply part of what it means to be human, a cycle that life presents us with. Taking care of ourselves and rebuilding that pillar of support we learned from our people is essential to living a full life without them.

It isn't work that can be monetized or quantified, and as a society, we do not value the work that healing from grief or trauma requires. We simply do not value care. No one is going to give you a prize, a raise, a medal, or a promotion for taking the time you need to care for yourself after a significant loss. Furthermore, therapy, acupuncture, time off from work, yoga, a vacation—all can be costly. We all need to do the work to ensure that healing after loss, that proper self-care, is a right and not a privilege. Even if it is just taking a few minutes out for yourself each day to get quiet and identify that deeper need, fight for that time. Find room for it. And if you are someone who is privileged enough to be able to access all of these things with ease, fight to ensure others can access them as well. And know that not everyone will support you as you do the work required to comfort and soothe and care for your body and mind after it's been battered by loss. You must do this work anyway because, without it, it is impossible to move to a place where you can honor what you've lost in a way that brings you peace and joy.

As I learned not only to acknowledge but also to honor my fragility, to press pause on a lifelong dream to become a mother in order to mother myself, I realized that care is the bridge to joy. After loss, we must take stock of what we truly need and access those things. Once I started to focus on my physical, emotional, and psychological needs, I started to feel better. Not great; I was still angry and sad and trying to recover from this loss amid a global pandemic, but better. In loving myself, in mothering myself, I found myself more able to access bits of joy. I realized that you cannot live a full life after death without taking real care of yourself. Your body, mind, and soul will tell you what kind of care you need, and when they do, respond. It is the only way to move through loss intact and capable of true, unbridled joy.

8

And . . .

I AM PRETTY SURE the rudest thing I've ever done is laugh at my mother's funeral. After dry swallowing a Xanax in the church rectory and just before I became a hysterical, sobbing mess as they closed her casket, I laughed, out loud, in the front row of Fishkill Baptist Church. I tried to stifle my giggles, which then became that aggressive form of silent laughter that produces tears. I laughed with my sister and cousin, and then my grandmother, who was trying to convince the three of us to stop laughing as she snickered silently alongside us. And to be clear, it wasn't rude because it was happening at my mother's funeral; it was rude because we were actively laughing at someone else. At the time, my family's church was predominantly white. I knew from my conversations with my mother that she wanted the classic gospel hymn "His Eye Is on the Sparrow" sung at her funeral. In my humble opinion, that song can only be sung well by a Black person, or maybe someone white like Kelly Clarkson who sounds super soulful, but it cannot be sung by just anyone. I had politely but firmly conveyed this message to our white pastor, Pastor Bob, and he said he had the perfect person in mind, a Black woman friend of his who was an excellent singer. When this woman started singing at my mother's funeral, I thought I might die myself. It was honestly remarkable how bad she was. She was just *so* bad; she butchered the song. She was completely off-key, and it was incredibly awkward. I've never heard anything like it before or since that day, and at that moment, in the middle of my sadness and despair, all I could do was laugh. It was that absurd. Here I was trying to plan this perfect memorial service for my mother, and this woman was ruining it. I am confident that it was a gift from my mother; it would be like her to send us a moment of comic relief to give us all a break from our grief.

The day we buried my mother was the second-worst day of my life, the first being the day she died. Joy, happiness, good cheer all felt like distant memories. They felt like something I'd lost when she died. I had no idea how to return to a place of lightness, of laughter, so my mom sent me a reminder that I could still laugh even though she was gone. She knew that even in the darkest times, we can still laugh; we can still smile. Those are the times we need it the most. It doesn't mean your pain has been erased. It doesn't mean everything has gone "back to normal." Smiles and laughter may feel uncomfortable because it may seem like you are moving on or forgetting about your person, like the world is moving on too fast from our pain, too far beyond your person's death. But it only means that you're learning how to live with loss. My friend the poet Maggie Smith calls it "the andness of things." Emotions are not just black and white, good and bad, either or. Most days we get a little bit of both. Living with loss requires you to embrace the sad feelings that sometimes come with the good things your person isn't around to share with you, as well as the joy you experience independent of grief. It is about getting comfortable with the "and" of your emotions. It is about being honest about your feelings and the duality of it all, even if your feelings don't align with the expectations of others. It is embracing the sorrow and joy you experience on your wedding day because your loved one isn't there. It is telling the truth when you finally become a mom that you're overjoyed and sad that your mom isn't here with you. It is about embracing with equanimity whatever comes up for you forever, no matter how out of place it may seem, like the aforementioned funeral giggle fest.

You can laugh, and still be just okay. Laughter does not mean happiness, and it does not mean that you're not grieving. What was normal or expected before your person died is not the same after they are gone. Laughter, or even moments and feelings of joy, don't remove the experience you're having with grief. That is the lie that our grief tells us. Death requires you to reconfigure your expectations around pleasure and joy. Things that previously only brought you joy—a promotion, getting your nails done, or watching a football game—may be tinged with sadness or nostalgia because your partner, mother, or son isn't there with you. Death asks us to acknowledge our loss forever, and sometimes that means otherwise joyful moments are complicated by feelings of grief. A beautiful sunset, playing with children, sitting on the beach, listening to nature—you're allowed to still feel the beauty of life, *and* you can miss your person. You can even feel joy while yearning to have them there with you. I just want you to know that this is okay. I want you to feel joy. I won't add to the chorus of people telling you that "they would want you to be happy," but I will say that I believe joy, happiness, and goodness are required in life, even after loss.

When I met Matt, I knew early on that he would become my husband. After years of dating Matt and surviving life in a studio apartment and adopting a dog, I was extra sure this was my guy. After the death of a loved one, you start to consider early on all the things they will miss out on, often focusing on the major milestones: graduations, weddings, births. As I've said, when I thought of marrying Matt, I always thought about the fact that my mother wouldn't be there, and an otherwise perfect day would likely be bittersweet. What I failed to account for was how much I might notice her absence in the lead-up. As soon as we got engaged, my anxiety mounted. I knew it wasn't because I didn't want to marry Matt, but it took a few months for me to realize this was grief. Like an uninvited guest, my grief showed up to the wedding early. I remember one day picking a fight with Matt because he just didn't care enough about the deal I found on wedding napkins. It was cheaper to buy them and donate them later than it was to rent them with the rest of our wedding dinner items. I was so proud of myself, but I have no idea why I thought he was going to give a shit about my wedding napkin victory. I realized, as I sat down to map out the details of our wedding day—seating charts, flowers, farm-to-table everything, custom invitations designed using a vintage map of the Hudson Valley—that is where my mother's death suddenly felt like an open wound. I realized after "Operation Napkingate" that no one else was going to care half as much as my mother would care about the little details surrounding our wedding. Of course I felt her absence most acutely in the details she had raised me to care about. She taught me that is where love lives, in the details, in the little things that make the big things extra special. Not having her there to do these little things with me took some of the joy out of it.

On the other hand, I actually did enjoy every single second of my wedding, from the moment I woke up until my new husband found me scarfing down leftover pasta at three a.m., with my bare hands, in the walk-in fridge in the catering kitchen at our wedding venue. Surprisingly, I walked down the aisle feeling like my mom was there. That day there was no grief for me, just moments of reflection in which I was filled with gratitude for who this woman raised me to be. There was no longing as I had felt at other times. On that date, all I could feel was her there. I think her physical absence that day was harder for other people, namely my new husband and my father, than it was for me. I knew she was there that day, and I was filled with an overwhelming sense of love.

In the context of grief, I tend to think of joy in three buckets: the joy you experience independent of grief, the joy that arises in the midst of grief, and the bitterness that comes in otherwise joyful moments because of all that you've lost.

I do understand that you might be reading this and not feeling any of this right now, because it is often hardest to access joy in the midst of grief. I'm not here to lie to you about joy. I don't believe in making lemons into lemonade or any other form of toxic positivity. An overwhelming wave of sorrow immediately followed my bout of laughter at my mother's funeral. When I realized at the end of the funeral, when they'd closed the casket, that that would be the last time I would ever see my mother's actual face, I broke. I shifted from laughter to inconsolable sobs. I was the last person to leave the church by my sheer insistence. I begged them to let me watch them close the casket. It was like I had to visually experience the finality of my mother's earthly existence.

Joy can sometimes feel impossible to access. On most days, joy can feel out of reach for some people. The task of having to strive for a joyful life after the death of a loved one isn't something that you want to hear after your loss. And I absolutely do not advise a "fake it till you make it" approach.

It may seem counterintuitive, but to access your joy, you must sit with your grief while allowing natural moments of respite from it. Somewhere in the middle of feeling absolutely miserable, you may find something that makes you smile, laugh, or experience a tiny bit of comfort. You need to accept the shittiness of the present moment in order to experience joy in any form. Laughing at my mother's funeral did not take away the pain of my loss. She had only been dead for four days. Laughing didn't make any of my pain go away, but it did give my brain a temporary and necessary brief break from my grief.

Accessing joy or having fun, especially in those early days after your person's death, may seem absurd, but on some days it might be what you need. When I first returned to my apartment in New York after losing my mother, all I was thinking about was survival. I had to remind myself to eat and take medication to sleep. I was wildly anxious and depressed, and I just kept asking myself, "How am I going to get through this? Am I going to get through this?" Those were the two questions running through my brain twenty-four hours a day. I didn't have any answers. I wasn't ready to talk about my grief or share memories of my dead mother with my friends or family. I hadn't even begun to process my loss, and I was barely thinking straight. I needed a break from it all, but I didn't even know how to express that. My friend Matt (not future husband Matt) insisted on taking me out to a bar we all loved at the time, a loud and rowdy spot, the kind of place that made serious conversations impossible. I was not ready to go out to a bar. It felt wrong. I knew I was sad; I missed my mom terribly, and I kind of just wanted to be left alone in my misery. He insisted, and then when we got there, he proceeded to do a "Stuntman Shot," which I had never seen before. He snorted salt, took a shot of tequila, and then squirted lime in his eye. I laughed out loud at his absurd and childish behavior, and it is admittedly one of the only memories I have of my first days back in New York after my mother died. His foolishness was exactly what I needed that night. Similar to when my friend Chris forced me to go to the movie, moments of respite from grief, brief bouts of laughter, can be an important aspect of our healing journey.

In the days following our pregnancy loss, I was not looking for joy. I wanted to sit with the pain, inhale all of what I was experiencing physically and mentally. I wasn't ready for distractions of any kind, so I took my own advice and just sat with my grief. All I wanted was for my pain to be validated. I didn't want anyone dragging me out and trying to convince me to have a good time. I wanted to watch *This Is Us*, about a family who lost their father, and eat Annie's mac and cheese and fruit snacks. I wanted to be left alone. I wanted to cry until I gave myself a headache. And if that's where you are right now, that is okay. How did I know that this was not the time to call a friend and head out to the bar, to mimic the relief I experienced when my friend Matt took me out? There is an interiority to experiencing joy in the midst of grief. Joy during this time has to be genuine. It can only be genuine if you are willing to open yourself up to it. The laugh at my mom's funeral was completely genuine; it was too ridiculous not to laugh. With Matt, I didn't know I needed a laugh, but I did know I needed a break, and that created an opening for him to provide a laugh. Only you will know for sure if today is a day when you're willing to be distracted by someone else's silliness, or if you need to just Netflix and cry all day long. Grief removes a fair amount of emotional certainty that you've depended on your entire life, where weddings always make you happy or your birthday is the best day of the year or a new professional opportunity is guaranteed to bring joy and gratitude and pride. You no longer have the clarity or certainty you once counted on around how something "good" might make you feel. Grief will sometimes force you to take a step back in an otherwise joy-filled moment, where you have to acknowledge feelings that you wish weren't there. Just as joy after loss cannot be faked, it also cannot be forced.

You are worthy of joy. And not in the "your person would want you to be happy" sort of way, which is probably true but annoying to hear on repeat. You deserve joy simply as a living and breathing human being. You deserve joy, even if it is at times tinged with grief. Your joy is as deserving as a child's—the most innocent of us all. When was the last time you went sledding? You deserve that kind of joy too. Spending an anniversary of my mother's death with my niece JJ opened my eyes to moments of joy that, even thirteen years later, I didn't know I needed and could never have accessed on my own.

If you ask those who knew my mother what they remember most about her, they will tell you about her smile, how she was always happy and smiling, and not in a forced, smiling-through-the-pain kind of way, but in a way that was genuine and full of love. She was sick often and honest about her struggles. She never complained, but she would tell you if she was having a bad day. In this environment, I was raised to find joy and gratitude amid heartache, and independent of it. She never felt guilty for being happy or joyful no matter what was happening around her or to her. She knew joy was essential to her survival and any ounce of healing.

Joy may feel like an indulgence, but it is not. Joy is a basic right. Don't feel cast aside from your grief; you need to entitle yourself to the joy you deserve. If you are going to live a full life after loss, you have to find your way back to joy. Through all of her physical pain, my mom was able to access joy because she was intentional about it. Joy doesn't have to be about a fancy vacation or anything big or expensive. Experiencing joy for most people is often in the simplest things. For my mom, holiday shopping started during the end of summer Labor Day sales. Christmas cookies were baked the day after Thanksgiving. Planning for birthday celebrations began months in advance, and there were always a handful of summer parties in the works as soon as the ground began to thaw in New York. She didn't have a lot financially, but she saved little bits of money throughout the year to fund her joy, which generally centered around celebrations and giving to others. She did whatever she needed to make it happen, even if making it happen simply involved sitting in a wheelchair, or even a hospital bed, bossing the rest of us around. She understood on a cellular level that no matter how hard life is, no matter how much grief or trauma you're forced to manage, life is still meant to be lived. My mom literally died laughing. Her commitment to joy is my inheritance.

Do not feel like you are betraying your person by experiencing joy. Experiencing joy is one of the many ways you can continue to love them.

9

. . . Legacy

When my mother was dying, the thing I feared most was how her death would change me. What was going to happen to me on the other side of this tragedy? Would it completely upend and alter my sense of self? I feared losing her would change how I saw the world and my place in it. During the final weeks and months, I felt like I was losing my identity. Up until that point, I had been at least partially defined by my mother, her illnesses, and my role as caretaker. Who would I be once she was gone? This is the part of death that I wanted to run the farthest from. We all do. However, I failed to understand that the death of a loved one, of someone you hold dear, *should* change you. That is their mark on the world. *You* are their mark on this world. In order for you to become someone's legacy when they die, you are required to change. Your transformation is their legacy. Your transformation, your change in perspective, the myriad of other ways in which you know you are no longer the same because your beloved father, adoring wife, hilarious best friend, or younger brother are no longer here: that is their legacy. You are their legacy.

When I was first grieving the loss of my mother, I didn't know how to think about this idea of legacy. I often found myself confusing her legacy with the idea of honoring her or keeping her memory alive externally, out in the world. We tend to conflate these different concepts, which leads to a lot of confusion around what to do and how to keep your person alive. Legacy is deeply personal and solely about you. I am my mother's legacy in a way that is different from my sister, who is also my mother's daughter, and an extension of her legacy. Her legacy is how I choose to live as a result of her life and death. That's something only I can own. We often work ourselves up over external elements of honoring our lost loved ones, things we can do like an honorarium or charity in their name. Those are things that some of us have the privilege to do out in the world, but a true and lasting legacy is really about love. It's internal. Legacy is based on the fact that there was someone you loved dearly and who loved you back, and that love now lives on through you.

As you sort through how to honor your lost loved one, think about how you have been changed by their life and their love to ensure they live in the hearts and minds of others from beyond the grave, through you. It's not a requirement or obligation; it's about what you really want to do that enables you to bring the person you lost back to life. What did you two like to do together? What about your relationship or how they treated you do you miss most? What did you learn from them? Consider identifying and embracing the things that bring you closer to your person. Identifying those things is a lifelong journey. Some you might identify right away, and others will take years to unfold, and that's okay. Grief is a lifelong journey; you can take as long as you want or need to figure out how you want to honor them. That's the beauty of honoring, of valuing a life; your person can continue to grow and expand through you.

In the days immediately following the death of someone you love, you are usually called upon to host a party. People might call it a funeral, a home-going, or a memorial service, but it is basically a party. A party with preplanned and prescribed rituals and maybe religious elements and outfits to select. I think of it as a slightly less expensive wedding. Folks may lead you to believe that this is how you honor them: by planning the perfect memorial service. As I've confessed, I was obsessed with my mother's funeral. As a planner and lover of parties, I threw myself into it because it was the one thing about death that I could understand. I had this indelible image in my mind of Jackie Kennedy at JFK's funeral procession. She is standing tall with her children at her side, a black veil covering her face, hands gloved, face stoic and expressionless as her husband's casket passes them. That is the image of grief, of honor, that I wanted and that I felt my mother deserved. Her memorial service had to be beautiful, graceful, and elegant. I wanted to be Jackie: tall, proud, and strong. I thought too much emotion or vulnerability was deeply unattractive and inappropriate. This was 2008, and I went back in time to 1963 and held tight to a completely dated vision of strength and poise, but at the time it worked for me. On March 1, 2008, we had a beautiful homegoing service for my mother. Her funeral included the custom programs my friends designed and printed, a slide show created by my more tech-savvy college roommate Adriana that featured songs from Stevie Wonder and John Legend, and a eulogy delivered by yours truly, which received a round of applause. I wore a custom outfit from the hit TV show *Gossip Girl*, with perfect nails, four-inch heels, and at least a pound of pearls. I firmly believe both my mama and Jackie Kennedy were proud. The service was beautiful, a massive success, and then it was over, and I felt hollow.

The truth is, there may not be such a thing as the perfect memorial. Many people don't have the means—whether financial or some other—to mimic a presidential passover, but more importantly, a memorial can in no way ever come close to reflecting the love you experienced with your person. I thought my mother's memorial service was the one time, or final time, I would get to celebrate her publicly. I wanted to get it right because I love her. Some people, especially those who've lost loved ones to COVID, didn't even get to attend their loved one's funeral, or maybe they didn't get to plan it, or plans they had were canceled because of the pandemic. Folks were forced to host parking lot funerals over Zoom, unable to physically comfort one another or memorialize their person according to their wishes. I had to attend my cousin Ebonee's funeral via Facebook Live, unable to be with my family due to pandemic travel restrictions, and it was horrific. There was grief in not being able to do things "our way." There was grief in not being able to comfort my mom's baby sister the way I would have liked to. There was grief over not being able to memorialize Ebonee publicly and in person the way we would have liked to. Ebonee was a big personality, and we all experienced our own personal brokenheartedness at not being able to say farewell on our terms. Even under "normal" grief circumstances, there's a lot of weight and long suffering between families during this time. As you move further away from your loss, you will identify a myriad of other moments when you can celebrate and memorialize your person, and the most prominent will be through your own life. When the fog has cleared, you will have an opportunity to focus on life again—their life and yours.

My cousin was a writer. I think of her often when I sit down to write. She was the eldest child in her family, and on October 24, 2020, she became my aunt's third child to die. She was very close to her mother and very much a "boss," so I honor her and my own mom by doing what I can for my aunt from afar. Even with all the grief I've experienced, I simply cannot imagine losing three of my children. I do what I can to show up for my aunt, sending flowers, ordering groceries, encouraging her to seek out a therapist, and it makes me feel closer to both my mother and Ebonee. When it comes to honoring a lost loved one, build your own playbook. Don't assume you have to do certain things a certain way or in a certain period of time.

Personally, I've found that there is something about the immediate post-death rituals and events that feels performative. No matter how much time, energy, or care one puts into the memorial, I've never met someone who thought it gave them a meaningful sense of long-term closure. Most people who have planned or attended funerals feel like it is something "you have to do," as opposed to something they innately wanted to do. Of course, if a close friend or relative passes away, you should attend out of respect for them and for your relationship. It is also really hard to think far beyond when you're in the early stages of grieving, about how to contribute to keeping them alive after death. But at some point, you begin to realize that you have the opportunity to include your lost loved one in your life forever. Truly, how you keep someone alive after death is deeply oriented around values and feeling more at peace on a daily basis. Choosing to live the values your loved one subscribed to is often the most genuine way to honor them. As we've discussed, I create holidays and events that center on my mom's spirit and values externally. My mother was the Queen of Christmas. Our house was decorated the day after Thanksgiving, with Christmas china sitting on the one table we had to eat dinner at every night between Thanksgiving and Christmas. We literally had to move the place settings daily to align with her vision for how grandly the holidays should be celebrated. No matter how much money we had or how sick she was, the whole spectacle was completely over the top. I struggled with Christmas after she died, but eventually, with the help of Matt, I found my way. Every year, as I mentioned earlier, we host an over-the-top holiday party called "Tacos and Baby Jesus." We serve multiple kinds of tacos, do a homemade cookie swap, host a charity food drive, and give out prizes for the most outrageous costumes. You wouldn't believe what some folks will put on just to win a semidecent bottle of wine.

Take the time to identify the things that bring you solace and really do bring your loved one back to life in some form or fashion. This also applies to their stuff. The week after my mother died, we got rid of, donated, or gave away the vast majority of her belongings and completely redecorated the bedroom she shared with my father. It forced me to decide early on what things of my mother's I wanted to keep. What really mattered to me? What would draw me closer to her now that she was dead? In the end, I kept a small pile of items: her "Harvard Mom" T-shirt, the dress she wore on her last vacation that we selected together, a pink cashmere sweater that we traded back and forth, and a jacket designed by my friend Abigail that she loved dearly. I wanted things I could touch that would immediately bring me back to my mama. Things that allow me to access who she was in life.

At its core, you serving as someone's legacy is all about authenticity and connection. What feels right to you? What brings you a sense of comfort? What about your relationship with your person was uniquely yours? What about their values did you always admire? Your grief is yours alone, and so is your role as someone's living legacy. Take the time to identify how someone's life, and their subsequent death, has transformed you. My mother's death initially made me a harder person. I was all sharp edges, and I moved through the world carrying the heaviness of grief, the heat of my rage, a deep-seated belief that I was all alone, and a fear of death. If I also die at forty-nine, what might I regret doing or not doing? And I was deeply lonely. In my mother's absence, I just didn't feel like I had anyone who loved me unconditionally the way she had. I had an amazing community, but I truly believed no one fully understood my experience and how much pain I was in. In retrospect, I am not sure any of these things are true, but this was how my mother's death initially left its mark on my life. As I worked through the grief and began to access with consistency the things that I needed to heal and process my loss, I began to recognize that her death actually made me softer. My loss gave me a deeper sense of empathy and understanding for others. It even made me a teeny tiny bit more patient. No one ever has or ever will describe me as patient, but death gave me a new sense of time. I felt urgency to live my life on my terms because I now understood time is all we have. My urgency is now balanced by a commitment to wait patiently for the things that really matter for the exact same reason. I felt my mother calling me to do big things and to stay focused on those big things and ignore distractions even when achieving the big things takes longer than I want it to. This made the pregnancy loss all the more devastating. I felt like I had waited, I had been patient, I had done all the things I was supposed to do, and it still hadn't worked out. In the aftermath, I was forced to ask myself whether or not it was something I still wanted. And once I realized the answer was yes, I doubled down on my commitment to becoming a mother. I didn't know what the path forward would look like, but I knew it was meant for me. That was the legacy my embryo left behind.

If you had asked me after my mother died how I was going to memorialize her, how I would include her in my life, I probably would have talked about the breast cancer charity I founded in her honor or her amazing funeral, but the further you get from the death of your person, the way you choose to memorialize them and their legacy becomes so much more personal than that. And personal doesn't necessarily mean private, but it does mean unique, authentic, and intentional. My friend Katy Rose started an Instagram account focused on cooking after she lost her dad because that is where she found him: in the kitchen. She found solace and community connecting with others who experienced grief and felt a connection between their lost loved ones and food. My roommate from college, Lizzie, lost her mother right after we graduated. Her mother, Sylvia, was a science teacher who had a particular fondness for butterflies, specifically monarchs. Lizzie takes her kids on nature walks, and they go butterfly hunting and talk about Sylvia. My friend Jillian, who lost her father when we were in middle school, still has one of his chairs. It sits in her son's bedroom, and this little guy who has never met her father calls it Grandpa's chair. I know someone who took the daffodil bulbs from her dead grandmother's yard and she and her daughters transplanted them in their yard. These are the things that bring my friends a deep sense of peace. These actions keep them authentically connected to their loved ones, and they are uniquely theirs. They aren't performative or based on religion or ritual; they are about their version of the love they shared with someone who is no longer here.

Because my mother loved holidays, I send out Mother's Day cards to other people's mothers. It is my way of keeping my mom's memory alive. I find her in other people, and I use Mother's Day to tell them that. That said, you will never find me going out for brunch on Mother's Day weekend because that is still triggering fourteen years later. That is the other thing about legacy: you don't just get to decide what you want to do. You can also establish fixed and firm rules around what isn't for you.

The cemetery has never been for me. My mom passed away over a decade ago, and I think I've only been to her grave about ten times. I only really started going after meeting Matt. I felt like I needed somewhere to bring him, but that's just not where I find my mother. But my father goes there every other week, maybe more frequently, and that is okay too. My parents took their wedding photos at the cemetery where my mother is buried. It is a beautiful cemetery. For him, it doesn't just represent sadness and death, but also love.

You can have access to your person's life. To bring them back to life, to bring yourself closer to who they were, the version of them that was still untouched by death, is all about getting closer to who they were at their best, their brightest, their most loving, by integrating those aspects of their character, their values, the things you loved together, and their good deeds into our lives. You pull them forward and allow them to live beyond the grave by bringing them with you wherever you go.

You keep them alive by enabling them to continue to live through you and those you love—even those they have never met. It is not about living in the past or even living the life you think they would want for you. It is about finding ways to integrate them into your present and future.

I do my best by going all out for Matt's birthday like my mom used to do for me, giving him handwritten notes and cards like the ones she used to send me, and making some version of her roast chicken at least once a month. I want Matt to experience her love even though he never met her. It requires a commitment to including my mother in our life. It takes a lot of imagination to envision these people who never met in a deep relationship with each other, but it really does work. When we bought a house, Matt insisted on planting my mother's favorite flowers, Stargazer lilies, in the yard. I protested for a year, claiming it would make me too sad, and then one spring, I said to Matt, "I have this great idea! We should plant some lilies out back." Being married also means I can have selective memory and take credit for my spouse's ideas. Every spring, when my lilies start to bloom, I smile, thinking of my mother. I also roll my eyes, knowing that Matt was right all along.

When you lean into who your person was at their core, when you know you are exemplifying the best of their values and the impact of their life and death, that is when you feel the most fulfilled and the most connected to them. When we can bring their spirit, their essence, back to life, we keep our people alive, letting them continue to live through us and those we love.

10

Love . . .

Love doesn't die. Love endures forever.

Your mother, your father, your brother, your wife, your best friend, whoever you lost still loves you, and their inability to act on that love is why we grieve. Those of us left behind are asked to manage the pain of unrequited unconditional love. Love that is never returned in the way we want it to be by the people we've lost. This is the source of our pain. The greater the love, the greater the pain. Fundamentally, love is both action *and* feeling. It serves as the foundation for our most important and secure attachments. We love our parents, our spouses, and our friends because of the way they treat us. Their actions to care for us, to support us, translate into feelings of love. When they die and stop being able to engage with us in the same way, what happens to all of that love? Does it just disappear? No.

Love doesn't die, and that is why we grieve. You don't get over love. Loving someone and being loved in return leaves an indelible imprint on your brain. It cannot be erased, because love can't be taken away, can't be taken back, even if our person is no longer with us in this world. Death forces us to continually recalibrate our expectations around love. The foundation of a full life after loss is love. It is choosing to continue to love your person in the present tense. It is moving forward with life, bringing them with you. It is deciding how to love them and how to continue to experience their love forever.

We are conditioned to view death as the end of the story, but that's a half-truth. Death is also a beginning. It's the beginning of your life without your person physically beside you here on earth, *and* it's also the beginning of a new relationship with your person. Death asks us to figure out how to pull them forward, how to bring them into a new future with you.

That commitment to finding a way, to accessing the things to heal, launched my quest years ago to understand the true nature of grief. I needed to understand why our losses cause so much pain, but also what we do about it. In the summer of 2020, I found my answer in an unexpected place: the pain of racism.

The day after George Floyd's murder, Matt found me curled up in a ball on the floor of my office, sobbing uncontrollably, unable to process his death and the burden of Blackness. In the days that followed, I found myself obsessing over the relationship between grief and love. My mother's love for me, my love for her, the grief experienced in my quest to become a mother, and the love Black people have been crying out for generations. Begging for a country that once recorded our value in ledgers alongside cattle and horses to acknowledge our grief and show us the love we deserve. The rallying cry Black Lives Matter is fundamentally rooted in an absence of love. I thought about how much I love being Black and how much grief, anxiety, and fear being Black sometimes brings. No matter what I do, no matter how much I love my country, my country continues to give me things to grieve. As I witnessed our nation's "racial reckoning" amid the backdrop of a disproportionate rise in COVID-19 deaths in the Black community thanks to systemic racism, I mourned.

As I gave myself space to grieve, I found myself unable to separate my questions about grief and survival from love. I regularly yearned for the love and support of my mother during those painful months of death, disease, racial uprising, and isolation. As I contemplated the nature of Black grief in particular, I wound up in a public conversation on Instagram with Sybrina Fulton, the mother of Trayvon Martin. Sybrina suffered deep personal grief as a direct result of racism and white supremacy when her son was killed by a white vigilante in 2012. During our chat, when I asked her how she continues to cope with her loss, Sybrina said, "I still love my son, and I know my son still loves me." Her use of the present tense was jarring to me. I knew my mom *loved* me, and I *loved* my mom, but I wondered to myself, could I carry that love into the present tense? And is love the path to resiliency after death? Instead of getting over it, we stay in it. We keep loving our people in the present tense, and that is how we live with the pain of loss. And for Black people, loving ourselves, deeply loving ourselves no matter what, is how we live with the pain of racism. Grief is love, and love is the antidote to grief.

In retrospect, it all feels painfully obvious. Of course I still love my mother in the present tense; that's why I miss her so damn much. And of course she still loves me; in death, she is still my mother, and I am still her child. The unconditional love we share with others does not end; if anything it grows. And that's why none of this is meant to be overcome. This is why there are no time lines or properly ordered steps. Love isn't something you conquer or control, and neither is the ensuing pain of loss. Both are simply meant to be lived. It took me twelve years, a pregnancy loss, a pandemic, and a racial uprising to recognize that I am not in control of my grief or my love. I love who I love, and I grieve because I love. Love is not meant to be contained by death. Its strength defies the grave if we give ourselves permission to find it.

I find my mother and her love when I'm the best version of myself, when I'm kind and generous and loving and caring for others the way she cared for me. I find her in my husband's desire to follow the rules and do things the "right" way when I would rather rush through something. I find her love in my sister's generous spirit. I see her in my hilarious and joyful niece JJ, and I can always taste her memory whenever I bite into a perfectly constructed chocolate chip cookie. I find her within and without, and most of all, I find her in the water.

I know she lives in the water. I see us stuck in time in the swimming pool at what was once the IBM Country Club. The pool where she sat on the edge with me on her feet. The pool where she would kick her legs and send me flying through the air and into water. The pool where I will always be safe, carefree, and loved. She's in the Caribbean Sea off the coast of Puerto Rico, home of her ancestors. She is at Lake George, the site of one of our last family vacations. She is in the purity, the strength, the fluidity, and the life-sustaining power of water.

Just because I've found her and her love does not mean I live a life absent of the pain of grief. At the end of the day, her love, as real as it is, as present as it is, is still lacking because she isn't here with me. The pain we experience, whether surrounding the death of a loved one or life in a country that still views us as chattel, is the sting of unrequited love. It is the feeling of lack that comes when your love isn't returned the way you want it to be. My mother is with me every day. I can find her, I can call on her, I can ask her for advice, I can include her in my life in big and small ways, but I can't pick up the phone and call her. I can't hold her hand. I can't text her for her famous bread pudding recipe. Instead, I have to honestly acknowledge her absence, I have to let myself feel the impact of this life-changing loss, and I have to let myself grieve.

If you are a human being capable of love and all of the wonder, awe, and joy that come with it, then you are also capable of feeling a deep sense of loss, despair, and sorrow when someone you love crosses over into death. **Let yourself grieve.** Do not follow my instructions, but use this book to navigate and validate your own unique grief experience.

When all I want is to put my head in my mom's

lap and let her rub my back and tell me everything will be okay; when I feel frustrated or sick or just not like myself, and all I want is my mom, I close my eyes, inhale deeply, and go there. I'm back in my childhood home, in my parents' bedroom, with my head in her lap. It is not the same. It is imperfect, and I am not comforted the way I was as a child, but I can still feel her love. You can access their love, their energy indefinitely because it's in you. It hasn't gone away. Everything they poured into you over the years didn't die when they died.

But because it is not the same, because there is no replacement for the person you lost, you have to build up that love within yourself. It is the only way to continue to move forward. You have to ask yourself, what is required to live in the midst of loss today? What do I need in order to be okay without my dad, my daughter, my child? Their love is certainly still there, but their physical presence isn't, so what do you need to do for you to be okay when you can't run into their arms or reach for their hand?

Know that each day is different, and only you can answer that question. As you learn to live without their physical presence in the world, your love for them grows. Their absence on this Earth forces you to recognize just how much love existed between the two of you. You are better able to see after death all that they gave you in life. Your appreciation, your respect, your gratitude, and ultimately your love are all magnified as you are forced to repeatedly acknowledge the depth of your loss. As you reimagine your life without them, as you surrender over and over again to the impact your grief has on your life, as you learn to navigate the "andness" of your emotions, and as you figure out how to once again open your heart up to love someone else unconditionally, you become more and more aware of their life. You become increasingly cognizant of all they gave you. You understand at a deeper level just how much they truly love you.

Lay claim to their love. I spent a lot of time on the floor of my office crying thanks to the isolation of the pandemic. I was forced to simply be with my feelings, and I was miserable. There were no distractions to be found, and the world was full of sorrow. As I sat in this moment of deep personal and global grief, I decided to choose love. I committed to loving my mother in the present tense. I committed to continuing to hold love in my heart for this little bundle of cells that didn't make it. I committed to loving my Blackness in the midst of racism and white supremacy. Most importantly, I committed to loving myself as much as my mother loves me and as much as I love her. I decided to love all parts of myself, even the pieces I don't like as much, because that is what unconditional love requires. In the absence of my mother's loving actions, without her here to remind me to be kind to myself, to be patient with my body, and to stop acting as though I'm a machine, I needed to take responsibility for those things myself. For all of it. I realized I couldn't love myself unconditionally while also chastising myself for feeling too much, for crying too much, for my body taking too long to heal. That's just not how it works. I committed to embracing unconditional love for myself and my mother and, in the process, I realized that this is the deepest form of acceptance.

Accept that you do not physically have the deepest desires of your heart and hold those desires with love anyway. The people you so badly want to hold, you can almost touch them with your hands. The people whose absence causes you to occasionally mourn or to wail. Accepting that you cannot lay claim to these people you love dearly hurts, but unconditional love requires acceptance.

We accept that our spouse only listens to us 70 percent of the time, we accept that every single night our child will run through a list of questions and requests in order to delay bedtime, we accept the friend who always runs ten minutes late because you know she loves you, but how do we accept death? How do we quell the longing that seemingly never ceases?

You don't. The longing is your love, and love isn't

meant to be contained or quelled. The only thing that makes the longing more bearable is simply expecting it, and accepting it as a normal part of your life after death. There is nothing wrong with your feelings. You have to learn to support yourself, to soothe yourself, and to love yourself to the best of your ability. No matter how the world views or values you, you have to value yourself. You are worthy of the time and space that your grief requires forever. There is nothing wrong with you if you are still nursing a broken heart, and it's been years since your person's death. The only way you get to a place where grief and joy can exist simultaneously is by understanding that you are of value, that your feelings matter, and those feelings are worthy of expression. You will only allow yourself to access all of the things that healing requires if you truly value yourself. Many of us never access full healing because we allow others to determine our value. Do not do this. You deserve the space you need to heal even if the world tries to deny you.

Once you acknowledge your worth, surrender fully to your grief, and access the care you need to heal, you will find yourself able to deeply and intentionally love your person and feel their love for you in return. A space opens up in your heart, and even in the midst of this absence you will carry forever, you begin to feel whole. When you fully accept their absence, that hole can be filled with love. Sometimes love on its own, sometimes love with a side of grief, but love nonetheless. Continuing to feel their love will sustain you. Their love and the love you have for yourself is what will get you through the worst of your grief.

Let love buoy you.

Acknowledgments

My friend Liza likes to say, "The day before your life changes forever is just like any other day."

On an otherwise unremarkable Thursday, we received a phone call. The next day, after five years of waiting, hoping, and praying, we became the proud parents of a beautiful baby boy in less than twenty-four hours. I am writing this little addendum to my book on my iPhone as our son naps in what used to be my office. He is still only a few weeks old, and I still haven't fully processed the enormity of this blessing, but I already know that this is the most meant-to-be thing that has ever happened to me. I've never known this level of contentment before, and I could not be more grateful.

Our son arrived three weeks before my manuscript was supposed to be submitted to my editor. As you can imagine, I turned in my book incredibly late, and the fact that I turned it in at all is nothing short of a miracle. The combination of new-parent exhaustion and the demands of a newborn, which we prayed for but didn't exactly plan for, is not the environment I expected to be finishing my book in, but here it is!

You are holding this book thanks to God and a lot of talented and generous helpers. I know acknowledgments usually begin with professional thanks, but family comes first in this house, and I have to start with my husband. Matt, you are the most important thing that's ever happened to me. Your belief in me and my ability to do what I want, to go after the things I think I'm worthy of and meant to do, is a big part of what enabled this book. For years I talked about writing a book, and way before any agents came calling, you told me to get writing. Your love, encouragement, ability to challenge me, sense of humor, commitment to grieving alongside me, and, most recent, your dedication to fatherhood and your ability to handle the early mornings so I can sleep in are all invaluable. You are a gift, and I am so glad I get to spend this life loving you. Also, thank you for insisting we get a dog way before I was ready. Sadie is the world's greatest dog and the best writing companion a girl could ask for.

To my son, Bennett, thank you for making me a mother, for showing me just how big my heart really is, and for inspiring me with your love. You are my joy. And to everyone who made our dream of parenthood a reality, thank you. You know who you are, and we wouldn't be here without you. An extra special thank you to the amazing doulas, especially Amanda Watson, who helped us care for our son so I could sleep just enough to finish this book.

To my father, Sam, for showing me what "in sickness and in health" really means, for always having something ridiculous or hilarious to say, and for raising me to take what I want from life *and* have a good time doing it. To my sister, Heather, for being an example of resilience and courage in the face of adversity. Thank you both for giving me full license to tell my story, which inevitably included your story's, as well. I know Mommy is proud of the family we've cobbled together in her absence. Bennett is so lucky to have you both.

To my godparents, Andrea and Timmy Sayles, my cousin Courtney Amal, my grandparents, Sam and Lossie Lee, who are my ever-present reminder to keep going, our crew in Wisconsin, and the rest of my big extended family, thank you. To Bennett's honorary grandparents, the Honorable Marie Johns and Wendell Johns, thank you for nourishing us with your love and endless, delicious, meals.

To the friends who are indeed family. The women (and a few men) who've stood by me and shaped me and loved me through the hardest of times and the happiest moments. The crew who organized themselves when Bennett arrived and we truly didn't even know what we needed. To the folks who have always made me feel loved in grief and in joy. The people who expect to be fed at my house, who look out for invitations to over-the-top birthday and holiday celebrations. The people who have helped me find my mother's love and my love for myself. My high school crew: Allison Brownell Salzer, Lillian Lee Erhardt, and Subrina Jendrasiak. To my college roommates, who I will always refer to as roommates in the present tense: Naomi Ages, Alisha Moran, Gloriana Salgado, Bridget Marvinsmith, Seo Yun Yang, Adriana Cosgriff, Vivian Bertseka Lemmer, Liza Fitzpatrick, Falyne Chave, Elizabeth Cleary, and Danae Pauli. To Scott and Megan Quimby, Dan and Nicole Curran, Ari and Marissa Matusiak, and Dave and Tracie Wescott.

To the people who stood by me in my early grief when I was mostly at my worst: Liana Douillet Guzman, Katie McDonough, Katie Murphy Kornel, Kimmy Scotti Metzger, Jackie Scharnick, Alexa Lynch, Ben Andujar, Aaron Andujar, and, of course, my old boss Michael Velucci and his wife, Teresa Boyle Vellucci. Michael, I could not have survived without your patience, gentleness, and good humor. Thank you for all of the sushi, cocktails, laughs, and, most important, for pushing me out of New York and toward my new life in DC.

To my team. Wow. I could not have done this without a lot of professional help. First off, my editor, Krishan Trotman. Krishan, I wholeheartedly believe our mothers conspired to put us together. Your brilliance, gentleness, attention to detail, and commitment to patiently pushing me to clarify every single word and thoughtfully make each point in this book are what made this book great. I know I could not have done it without you. To the rest of the Hachette/Legacy Lit/Grand Central Publishing family, including but not limited to Amina Iro, Kathryn Gordon, and Abimael Ayala-Oquendo. I am so grateful for your hard work on this book. To my agent, Peter Steinberg, thank you for finding me and convincing me that I had a "big book" to write.

To my work "husband," Chris Cormier Maggiano, I could not have created a more intelligent, thoughtful, hardworking, or detail-oriented professional partner. Thank you for carrying extra work, for buying me all the treats/sweets/bourbon I needed while writing, and for always supporting me in my grief. I am so indebted to you. And thank you Chase Cormier Maggiano for being an amazing friend and for sharing your husband with me. I love you both dearly.

Thuraya Masri, you truly showed up right on

time. Thank you for lovingly reading every word of *both* versions of this manuscript and giving me honest feedback. You absolutely made this book better while simultaneously making the rest of my life easier. I couldn't have done it without you.

To Gabi Birkner, for helping me find my voice and providing endless edits and moral support. To Dr. Christy Denckla, for providing essential research to ensure this book isn't just about me but instead is grounded in the best bereavement data and information available. And to our mutual friend, Dr. Christopher Golden, for introducing us to each other.

To everyone who believed in this book and in my talent as a writer long before I did, but especially Alicia Menendez, Carlos Odio, Judee Ann Williams, Samantha Fuld, Michael Skolnik, Reshma Saujani, Joshua and Michelle Dubois, Anthony Hayes, Faith Cole, Jim Shelton, Willa Seldon, Willie and Christina Geist, Alex Elle, Jen Pastiloff, Elaine Welteroth, Mattie Kahn, Chloe Schama, Ella Riley-Adams, and Natasha Alford.

And I know this is a weird one, but if you know me well, you know I wrote most of this book while still managing complications from my underlying medical condition and my pregnancy loss. Thank you to the hardworking doctors, nurses, and, of course, therapists who helped me find solutions and ultimately the physical and mental health we all deserve: Emily Boland, Natalie Moore, Suchithra Nancherla, Lisa Cefalu, Matthew Churchill, and Lysa Phan. I am so grateful to each and every one of you.

To everyone who sent a kind word, care package, or thoughtful text, and to all the folks named in this book, thank you for inspiring and supporting me.

During this time, it feels imperative to say thank you to everyone who has worked hard to keep us safe during the COVID-19 pandemic. To every doctor, nurse, scientist, delivery person, and every other essential worker *and* their families, I am deeply grateful.

Lastly, to those who have lost loved ones this last year, to COVID or otherwise, this book is for you. I cannot imagine what it must feel like to endure death and grief in the midst of a global pandemic. I hope at a minimum my words serve to validate your pain and help you find your person's love.

With gratitude, hope, and love,

Marisa

Bibliography

Bonanno, G. A., Keltner, D., Holen, A., and Horowitz, M. J. "When Avoiding Unpleasant Emotions Might Not Be Such a Bad Thing: Verbal-Autonomic Response Dissociation and Midlife Conjugal Bereavement." *Journal of Personality and Social Psychology* 69 (1995): 975–989. https://doi:10.1037//0022-3514.69.5.975.

Boulware, D. L., and Bui, N. H. "Bereaved African American Adults: The Role of Social Support, Religious Coping, and Continuing Bonds." *Journal of Loss and Trauma* 21 no. 3 (2016): 192–202.

Briere, J., Agee, E., and Dietrich, A. "Cumulative Trauma and Current Posttraumatic Stress Disorder Status in General Population and Inmate Samples." *Psychological Trauma.* 8 no. 4 (July 2016): 439–446. https://doi: 10.1037/tra0000107. Epub PMID: 26752099.

Dohrenwend, B. S., and Dohrenwend, B. P. (Eds.). *Stressful Life Events: Their Nature and Effects.* John Wiley & Sons., 1974.

Ettman, C. K., Cohen, G. H., Abdalla, S. M., and Galea, S. "Do Assets Explain the Relation between Race/Ethnicity and Probable Depression in U.S. Adults?" PLoS One 15 no. 10 (2020): e0239618.

Geronimus, A. T., Hicken, M. T., Pearson, J. A., Seashols, S. J., Brown, K. L., and Cruz, T. D. "Do US Black Women Experience Stress-Related Accelerated Biological Aging?: A Novel Theory and First Population-Based Test of Black-White Differences in Telomere Length." *Human Nature* 21 no. 1 (2010): 19–38.

Keyes, K. M., Pratt, C., Galea, S., McLaughlin, K. A., Koenen, K. C., and Shear, M. K. "The burden of loss: unexpected death of a loved one and psychiatric disorders across the life course in a national study." *American Journal of Psychiatry* 171 no. 8(2014): 864–871.

Klass, D., Silverman, P. R., and Nickman, S. (Eds.). *Continuing Bonds: New Understandings of Grief.* Taylor & Francis, 2014.

Linehan, Marsha M. *Cognitive-Behavioral Treatment of Borderline Personality Disorder.* Guilford Publications, 2018.

O'Connor, M. F., Irwin, M. R., and Wellisch, D. K. "When Grief Heats Up: Pro-Inflammatory Cytokines Predict Regional Brain Activation." *Neuroimage* 47 no. 3 (2009): 891–896. Doi: 10.1016/j.neuroimage.2009.05.049. Epub 2009 May 27. PMID: 19481155; PMCID: PMC2760985.

Ong, A. D., Bergeman, C. S., and Bisconti, T. L. "The Role of Daily Positive Emotions during Conjugal Bereavement." *Journals of Gerontology Series B: Psychological Sciences and Social Sciences* 59 no. 4 (2004): P168–176. https://doi: 10.1093/geronb/59.4.p168. PMID: 15294920.

Petrie, K. J., Booth, R. J., and Pennebaker, J. W. "The Immunological Effects of Thought Suppression." *Journal of Personality and Social Psychology* 75 no. 5(Nov. 1998): 1264–1272. Doi: 10.1037//0022-3514.75.5.1264. PMID: 9866186.

Robinaugh, D. J. and McNally, R. J. "Remembering the Past and Envisioning the Future in Bereaved Adults with and without Complicated Grief." *Clinical Psychological Science* 1 no. 3 (2013): 290–300. https://doi:10.1177/2167702613476027.

Stroebe, M., and Schut, H. "The Dual Process Model of Coping with Bereavement: A Decade On." *Omega (Westport)* 61 no. 4 (2010): 273–289. https://doi:10.2190/OM.61.4.b. PMID: 21058610.

Stroebe, M., Finkenauer, C., Wijngaards-de Meij, L., Schut, H., van den Bout, J., and Stroebe, W. "Partner-Oriented Self-Regulation among Bereaved Parents: The Costs of Holding In Grief for the Partner's Sake." *Psychological Science* 24 no. 4 (Apr. 2013): 395 –402. https://doi: 10.1177/0956797612457383. Epub PMID: 23406609.

Umberson, D., Olson, J. S., Crosnoe, R., Liu, H., Pudrovska, T., Donnelly. R. "Death of Family Members as an Overlooked Source of Racial Disadvantage in the United States." *Proceedings of the National Academy of Sciences of the U.S.A.* 114 no. 5 (Jan. 31, 2017):

915–920. https://doi:10.1073/pnas.1605599114. Epub PMID: 28115712; PMCID: PMC5293066.

Williams, D. R., and Mohammed, S. A. "Discrimination and Racial Disparities in Health: Evidence and Needed Research. *Journal of Behavioral Medicine* 32 no. 1 (2009), 20–47.